Computer Concepts

FOURTH EDITION – ILLUSTRATED

BRIEF

Computer Concepts

FOURTH EDITION – ILLUSTRATED

BRIEF

June Jamrich Parsons / Dan Oja

COURSE TECHNOLOGY

THOMSON LEARNING

Australia • Canada • Mexico • Singapore • Spain • United Kingdom • United States

COURSE TECHNOLOGY
™
THOMSON LEARNING

Computer Concepts, Fourth Edition—Illustrated Brief

is published by Course Technology.

Contributing Author:
Rachel Biheller Bunin

Developmental Editor:
Pamela Conrad

Managing Editor:
Nicole Jones Pinard

Senior Product Manager:
Emily Heberlein

Production Editor:
Debbie Masi

Associate Product Manager:
Christina Kling Garrett

Editorial Assistant:
Elizabeth M. Harris

Interior Designer:
Betsy Young

Photo and Video Researcher:
Abby Reip

Composition:
GEX Publishing Services

Credits

Author Acknowledgements

I would like to offer my sincerest thanks to Dan Oja and June Parsons for entrusting me and the Illustrated team to adapt their groundbreaking, best-selling New Perspectives Concepts book into the Illustrated format. Without their comprehensive and exceptional content, I could not have created the Illustrated book you are reading today. Special thanks to Nicole Pinard, for having the vision three editions ago to let me create the first Concepts Illustrated book. It's been a wonderful adventure and I am grateful for the chance to work as the adapting author on this book, and see it into this Fourth Edition. My most heartfelt thanks and admiration go to Pamela Conrad, the Developmental Editor, who has worked with me on this project through all four editions. Her ability to see the big picture and keep all the details in check, while sharing new ideas, is awesome.

The Illustrated team is the best there is. Emily Heberlein contributed extraordinary leadership as the Project Manager, keeping all the components on track and providing insight and guidance throughout. Thanks to Debbie Masi; she is an unparalleled Production Editor and always stays calm and delivers above and beyond. Thanks to Kendra Neville and GEX for all their work and all those timely .pdf files. Thanks also to Abby Reip for finding those great photographs to bring this book to life. Thanks to our manuscript reviewers, Catherine Murphy, Barbara Cress, and Nancy Bogage for their insights and comments. On behalf of the entire Illustrated team, we hope you find this book a valuable resource for your students.

- Rachel Biheller Bunin, Adapting Author

We offer heartfelt thanks to all of the members of the Illustrated team for contributing their vision, talent, and skills to make this book a reality. Special thanks to Rachel Bunin for her fast and efficient work as the adapting author; Pamela Conrad for her insights as the developmental editor; Debbie Masi for her solid work as the Production Editor; Betsy Young for her beautiful new design; and Emily Heberlein for tracking all the bits and pieces of this project. Whether you are a student or instructor, we thank you for using our book and hope that you find it to be a valuable guide to computers and software.

- June Parsons, Dan Oja, and MediaTechnics for the New Perspectives Series

FIGURE No.

Unit A
Figure A-6: Courtesy of IBM Corporation
Figure A-9: Courtesy of Chris Conrad
Figure A-12: Courtesy of Microsoft Corporation
Unit C
Figure C-21: Courtesy of NASA
Figure C-25: Courtesy of Chris Conrad

Brief Contents

Contents

indicates students can explore the concept further by visiting the InfoWeb Links Web site at www.course.com/downloads/illustrated/concepts4

Preface

Welcome to Computer Concepts, Fourth Edition—Illustrated Brief. The Fourth Edition includes many enhancements and additions while preserving all of the best from the Third Edition. We've designed a **new interior look** to increase the accessibility and ease-of-use for the units, while preserving the **Illustrated two-page lesson format**. We've included **new unit features** to add flexibility for instructors and reinforcement for students. We've closely integrated the book with **all new information and links** on the InfoWebLinks Web site to provide extensive opportunities for student exploration. Icons throughout the book indicate when a student can go to the Web site for more. We've added a fourth unit to increase the amount of coverage. The resulting package is a fast-paced, engaging, and Web-enriched introduction to today's most cutting-edge computer concepts. Make sure you take a look at the Instructor's Resource Kit section in the Preface to learn more.

About the Illustrated Approach

What makes the information in this book so easy to access and digest? It's quite simple. As shown in this sample lesson, each concept is presented on two facing pages, with the main points discussed on the left page and large, dramatic illustrations presented on the right. Students can learn all they need to know about a particular topic without having to turn the page! This unique design makes information extremely accessible and easy to absorb, and makes a great reference for after the course is over. The modular structure of the book also allows for great flexibility; you can cover the units in any order you choose, and you can skip lessons if you like.

A single concept is presented in a two-page "information display" to help students absorb information quickly and easily

Easy-to-follow introductions to every lesson focus on a single concept to help students get the point quickly

Details provide additional key information on the main concept

---

UNIT B

Exploring CD/DVD technology

A CD-ROM drive is an optical storage device that is usually installed in one of the system unit's drive bays. **CD-ROM (compact disc read-only memory)** is based on the same technology as the audio CDs that contain your favorite music. Your computer can read data from a CD-ROM, but you can't store or record any of your own data on a CD-ROM disk. Two CD-writer technologies called CD-R and CD-RW allow you to create your own CDs. **DVD** ("digital video disc" or "digital versatile disc") is a variation of CD technology that was originally designed as an alternative to VCRs, but was quickly adopted by the computer industry to store data.

DETAILS

- A computer **CD-ROM disk**, like its audio counterpart, contains data that was stamped on the disk surface when it was manufactured. Today, when you purchase software from a computer store, the box typically contains CDs. Therefore, unless you plan to download all of your new software from the Internet, your computer should have a CD drive so that you can install new software. Figure B-11 shows how to place a CD in the drive. Figure B-12 illustrates how a CD-ROM drive uses laser technology to read data.

- CD-ROM technology provides a far larger storage capacity than floppy disks, Zip disks, or SuperDisks. A single CD-ROM disk holds up to 680 MB, equivalent to more than 300,000 pages of text. The surface of the disk is coated with a clear plastic, making the disk quite durable. Unlike magnetic media, the data on a CD-ROM is not susceptible to permanent damage by humidity, fingerprints, dust, or magnets.

- The original CD-ROM drives were able to access 150 KB of data per second. The next generation of drives doubled the data transfer rate and was consequently dubbed "2X"; and transfer rates are continually increasing. A 24X CD-ROM drive, for example, would transfer data at a rate of 24 × 150 KB, or 3,600 KB per second.

- A **CD-R (compact disc recordable)** drive records data on a special CD-R disk. The drive mechanism includes a laser that changes the reflectivity of a dye layer on a blank CD-R disk. As a result, the data on the disk is not actually stored in pits. Dark spots in the dye layer, however, play the same role as pits to represent data and allow the disks that you create to be read by not only a CD-R drive, but also by a standard CD-ROM or DVD

drive. The data on a CD-R cannot be erased or modified once recorded, but most CD-R drives allow you to record your data in multiple sessions.

- **CD-RW (compact disc rewritable)** technology allows you to write data on a CD and change that data at a later time. The process requires special CD-RW disks and a CD-RW drive, which uses phase change technology to alter the crystal structure on the disk surface. Altering the crystal structure creates patterns of light and dark spots similar to the pits and lands on a CD-ROM disk. The crystal structure can be changed from light to dark and back again many times, making it possible to record and modify data much like you can with a hard disk or a floppy disk. However, accessing, saving, and modifying data on a CD-RW disk is slower than on a hard disk.

- Both CD-R and CD-RW technologies are quite useful for archiving data and distributing large files. **Archiving** refers to the process of removing infrequently used data from a primary storage device to another storage medium, such as a CD-R.

- A computer's DVD drive can read disks that contain computer data (often called **DVD-ROM** disks) and disks that contain DVD movies (sometimes called DVD-Video disks). A DVD holds about 4.7 GB (4,700 MB), compared with 680 MB on a CD-ROM. Like a CD-ROM disk, a DVD-ROM disk is permanently stamped with data at the time of manufacture, so you cannot add or change data. The speed of a DVD drive is measured on a different scale than a CD drive. A 1X DVD drive is about the same speed as a 9X CD drive. Table B-1 provides additional speed equivalents.

Using DVD technologies

A computer DVD drive is not exactly the same as one that's connected to a television set. Even with the large storage capacity of a DVD, movie files are much too large to fit on a disk unless they are compressed, using a special type of data coding called MPEG-2. The DVD player that you connect to your television includes MPEG decoding circuitry, which is not included on your computer's

DVD drive. When you play DVD movies on your computer, it uses the CPU as an MPEG decoder. The necessary decoder software is included with Windows, or can be located on the DVD itself. You cannot play DVDs on your CD-ROM drive, but you can play CD-ROM, most CD-R, and most CD-RW disks on your DVD drive.

44 COMPUTER CONCEPTS

Icons in the margins indicate that an InfoWeb is featured for that lesson

News to Use boxes relate the lesson material to real-world situations to provide students with additional practical information

Large photos and screen-
shots illustrate the lesson
concepts

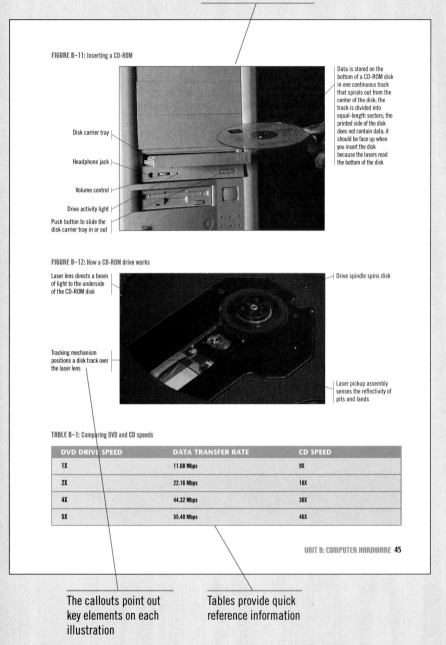

FIGURE B-11: Inserting a CD-ROM

Disk carrier tray

Headphone jack

Volume control

Drive activity light

Push button to slide the
disk carrier tray in or out

Data is stored on the
bottom of a CD-ROM disk
in one continuous track
that spirals out from the
center of the disk; the
track is divided into
equal-length sectors; the
printed side of the disk
does not contain data; it
should be face up when
you insert the disk
because the lasers read
the bottom of the disk

FIGURE B-12: How a CD-ROM drive works

Laser lens directs a beam
of light to the underside
of the CD-ROM disk

Drive spindle spins disk

Tracking mechanism
positions a disk track over
the laser lens

Laser pickup assembly
senses the reflectivity of
pits and lands

TABLE B-1: Comparing DVD and CD speeds

DVD DRIVE SPEED	DATA TRANSFER RATE	CD SPEED
1X	11.08 Mbps	9X
2X	22.16 Mbps	18X
4X	44.32 Mbps	36X
5X	55.40 Mbps	46X

UNIT B: COMPUTER HARDWARE **45**

The callouts point out
key elements on each
illustration

Tables provide quick
reference information

Unit Features

Each unit contains the following features, providing a flexible teaching and learning package.

- **InfoWebs** The computer industry changes rapidly.
  Students can get up-to-date information by exploring
  the concept on the InfoWebLinks Web site, when
  indicated by an InfoWeb icon. The site is located at
  www.course.com/downloads/illustrated/concepts4.

- **Tech Talk** Each unit ends with a Tech Talk lesson.
  These lessons go into greater depth on a technical
  topic related to the unit. Instructors have the option
  of assigning this section or skipping it, depending on
  the expertise of the students and the course goals.

- **Issue** It is important to keep abreast of issues that
  relate to technology. Each unit contains an interesting Issue article, followed by Expand the Ideas
  questions to encourage students to form and express
  their own opinions.

- **Key Terms** Students can use this handy list to review
  bold terms which represent key concepts from the unit.
  Definitions are provided in the glossary.

- **Unit Review** After completing the Unit Review,
  students will have synthesized the unit content in
  their own words.

- **Fill in the Best Answer** Students can complete this
  exercise to determine how well they have learned the
  unit content.

- **Independent Challenges** These exercises enable students to explore on their own and develop critical
  thinking skills. Challenges with an E-Quest icon point
  students to the Web to complete the exercise.

- **Visual Workshop** Based on a screenshot or illustration,
  Visual Workshops encourage independent thinking.

Instructor's Resources

The Instructor's Resource Kit (IRK) is Course Technology's way of putting the resources and information needed to teach and learn effectively into your hands. With an integrated array of teaching and learning tools that offer you and your students a broad range of technology-based instructional options, we believe this kit represents the highest quality and most cutting edge resources available to instructors today. Many of these resources are available at www.course.com.

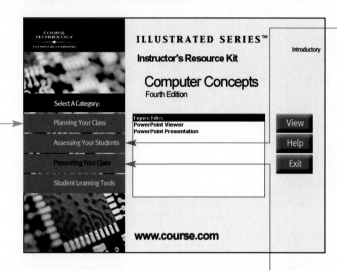

- **Select Assessing Your Students to open ExamView**—ExamView is a powerful testing software package that allows instructors to create and administer printed, computer (LAN-based), and Internet exams. ExamView includes hundreds of questions that correspond to the topics covered in this text, enabling students to generate detailed study guides that include page references for further review. The computer-based and Internet testing components allow students to take exams at their computers, and also save you time by grading each exam automatically.

- **Select Planning Your Class to use the Instructor's Manual and Sample Syllabus**—This enhanced Instructor's Manual offers an outline for each unit, lecture notes, extra assignments, and solutions to exercises to make incorporating the book, InfoWebs, teaching tools and assessment a snap! The Sample Syllabus provides a suggested outline that you can customize for your course.

- **Select Presenting Your Class to access the PowerPoint Presentations and Figure Files**—Presentations have been created for each unit to assist you in classroom lectures or to provide to students. All the figures from the book are also provided for your use in creating overhead transparencies or your own presentations.

Online Learning

We offer a full range of content for use with ClassAct, BlackBoard and WebCT to simplify the use of Computer Concepts in distance education settings, or to supplement your traditional class. Visit **www.course.com** for more information.

Before You Begin

 When you see an InfoWeb icon (shown to the left), you can access the latest information and explore the concepts in the book further by going to the InfoWebLinks Web site. To access this site, you'll need a Web browser and an Internet connection. If you can send e-mail and access the Web with your computer, you probably have such a connection. To access the Web site, simply type www.course.com/downloads/illustrated/concepts4 in the Address bar or Location bar of your Web browser.

If you are using your own computer, or if your computer lab allows you to make such changes, you can set the InfoWebLinks Web site as your browser home page by following these steps:

In Microsoft Internet Explorer:

1. Open the site at www.course.com/downloads/illustrated/concepts4
2. Click Tools on the menu bar, then click Internet Options
3. Click the Use Current button, then click OK

In Netscape:

1. Open the site at www.course.com/downloads/illustrated/concepts4
2. Click Edit on the menu bar, then click Preferences
3. Click Use Current Page, then click OK

If changing your home page is not an option, you can instead make the site easily accessible by adding it to your list of Favorites or Bookmarks (again, if you are using your own computer or your computer lab allows it).

To create this Favorite in Internet Explorer:

1. Open the site at www.course.com/downloads/illustrated/concepts4
2. Click Favorites on the menu bar, then click Add to Favorites
3. Click OK

To add this as a Bookmark in Netscape:

1. Open the site at www.course.com/downloads/illustrated/concepts4
2. Click the Bookmarks button under the Location text box, then click Add Bookmark

See your instructor or technical support person for help in connecting to the Internet or using your Web browser.

UNIT A
Computer and Internet Basics

OBJECTIVES

Define computers
Explore computer functions
Categorize computers
Examine personal computer systems
Explore data, information, and files
Introduce application and system software
Define Internet basics
Connect to the Internet
Understand World Wide Web basics
Use browsers
Understand e-mail basics
Tech Talk: The Boot Process

Unit A provides an overview of computer and Internet technologies. The unit begins by defining the basic characteristics of a computer system and then provides a quick overview of data, information, and files. You will be introduced to application software, operating systems, and platform compatibility. You will get a basic overview of the Internet, the Web, and e-mail. The unit concludes with a lesson on the boot process, the sequence of events that happens when you turn on your computer.

Defining computers

Whether you realize it or not, you already know a lot about computers. You've picked up information from commercials and magazine articles, from books and movies, from conversations and correspondence, and perhaps even from using your own computer and trying to figure out why it doesn't always work. This lesson provides an overview designed to help you start organizing what you know about computers, provide you with a basic understanding of how computers work, and get you up to speed with basic computer vocabulary.

DETAILS

- The word "computer" has been part of the English language since 1646, but if you look in a dictionary printed before 1940, you might be surprised to find a computer defined as a person who performs calculations! Prior to 1940, machines that were designed to perform calculations were referred to as calculators and tabulators, not computers. The modern definition and use of the term "computer" emerged in the 1940s, when the first electronic computing devices were developed.

- Most people can formulate a mental picture of a computer, but computers do so many things and come in such a variety of shapes and sizes that it might seem difficult to distill their common characteristics into an all-purpose definition. At its core, a **computer** is a device that accepts input, processes data, stores data, and produces output, all according to a series of stored instructions.

- A **computer system** includes hardware, peripheral devices, and software. Figure A-1 shows a basic computer system. **Hardware** includes the electronic and mechanical devices that process data. The term "hardware" refers to the computer as well as components called peripheral devices. **Peripheral devices** expand the computer's input, output, and storage capabilities.

- An **input device**, such as a keyboard or mouse, gathers input and transforms it into a series of electronic signals for the computer. An **output device**, such as a monitor or printer, displays, prints, or transmits the results of processing from the computer memory.

- A computer requires instructions called **software**, which is a **computer program** that tells the computer how to perform particular tasks.

- A **computer network** consists of two or more computers and other devices that are connected for the purpose of sharing data and programs. A **LAN (local area network)** is simply a computer network that is located within a limited geographical area, such as a school computer lab or a small business.

FYI

The term "personal computer" is sometimes abbreviated as "PC." However, "PC" is usually used for a specific type of personal computer that runs Windows software.

FIGURE A-1: A basic computer system

Exploring computer functions

To really understand computers, you can look at the functions they perform. Figure A-2 illustrates the basic computer functions—accept input, process data, store data, and produce output—and shows the components that work together to accomplish each function.

DETAILS

- Accept input. A computer accepts input. Computer **input** is whatever is put into a computer system. Input can be supplied by a person, by the environment, or by another computer. Examples of the kinds of input that a computer can accept include the words and symbols in a document, numbers for a calculation, pictures, temperatures from a thermostat, music or voice audio signals from a microphone, and instructions from a computer program.

- Process data. A computer processes data. In the context of computing, **data** refers to the symbols that represent facts, objects, and ideas. Computers manipulate data in many ways, and we call this manipulation **processing**. Some of the ways that a computer can process data include performing calculations, sorting lists of words or numbers, modifying documents and pictures, and drawing graphs. The instructions that tell a computer how to carry out the processing tasks are referred to as a **computer program**, or simply a "program." In a computer, most processing takes place in a **microprocessor** called the **central processing unit (CPU)**, which is sometimes described as the "brain" of the computer.

- Store data. A computer stores data so that it will be available for processing. Most computers have more than one location for storing data, depending on how the data is being used. **Memory** is an area of a computer that temporarily holds data waiting to be processed, stored, or output. **Storage** is the area of a computer that holds data on a permanent basis when it is not immediately needed for processing. For example, while you are working on it, a document is in memory; it is not in storage until you save it. After you save the document, it is still in memory until you close the document, exit the program, or turn the computer off. Documents in memory are lost when you turn off the power. Stored documents are not lost when the power is turned off.

- Produce output. **Output** consists of the processing results produced by a computer. Some examples of computer output include reports, documents, music, graphs, and pictures. An output device displays, prints, or transmits the results of processing. Figure A-2 helps you visualize the input, processing, storage, and output activities of a computer.

FIGURE A-2: Basic computer functions

A computer produces output.
You use an output device, such as a printer or display screen, to see the computer outputs—the results of processing

A computer processes data.
The CPU retrieves the numbers and the instruction, and then processes the numbers by performing addition; the result, 9, is temporarily held in memory; from memory, the result can be output or stored

A computer accepts input.
You use an input device, such as a keyboard, to input numbers, such as 2 and 7, along with the instruction ADD; the instruction and the numbers are temporarily held in memory

A computer stores data.
You can permanently store data on disks and CDs

Understanding the importance of stored programs

Early computers were really no more than calculating devices designed to carry out a specific mathematical task. To use one of these devices for another task, it was necessary to rewire or reset its circuits—a task best left to an engineer. In a modern computer, the idea of a **stored program** means that instructions for a computing task can be loaded into a computer's memory. These instructions can easily be replaced by different instructions when it is time for the computer to perform a different task. The stored program concept allows you to use your computer for one task, such as word processing, and then easily switch to a different type of computing task, such as editing a photo or sending an e-mail message. It is the single most important characteristic that distinguishes a computer from other simpler and less versatile devices.

Categorizing computers

Computers are versatile machines, but some types of computers are better suited to certain tasks than others. Computers are categorized to help consumers associate computers with appropriate tasks. Categorizing computers is a way of grouping them according to criteria such as usage, cost, size, and capability. Knowing how a computer has been categorized provides an indication of its best potential use. To reflect today's computer technology, the following categories are appropriate: personal computers, handheld computers, workstations, videogame consoles, mainframes, super-computers, and servers.

DETAILS

- A **personal computer**, also called a **microcomputer**, is designed to meet the computing needs of an individual. It typically provides access to a wide variety of computing applications, such as word processing, photo editing, e-mail, and Internet access. Personal computers include **desktop computers**, as illustrated in Figure A-3, and **notebook computers** (sometimes called "laptop computers"), as illustrated in Figure A-4. A desktop has separate components, while laptops have a keyboard, monitor, and system in one compact unit. Laptops are considerably more expensive than comparable desktops.

- A **handheld computer**, also called a **PDA (Personal Digital Assistant)**, shown in Figure A-5, is designed to fit into a pocket, run on batteries, and be used while you are holding it. A PDA is typically used as an electronic appointment book, address book, calculator, and notepad. Inexpensive add-ons make it possible to send and receive e-mail, use maps and global positioning to get directions, maintain an expense account, and make voice calls using cellular service. With its slow processing speed and small screen, a handheld computer is not powerful enough to handle many of the tasks that can be accomplished using desktop or notebook personal computers.

- Computers that are advertised as **workstations** are usually powerful desktop computers designed for specialized tasks such as design tasks. A workstation can tackle tasks that require a lot of processing speed, such as medical imaging and computer-aided design. Some workstations contain more than one micro-processor, and most have circuitry specially designed for creating and displaying three-dimensional and animated graphics. "Workstation" can also mean an ordinary personal computer that is connected to a local area network.

- A **videogame console**, such as the Nintendo® GameCube™, the Sony PlayStation®, or the Microsoft XBox®, is a computer. In the past, a videogame console was not considered a computer because of its history as a dedicated game device that connects

to a TV set and provides only a pair of joysticks for input. Today's videogame consoles, however, contain microprocessors that are equivalent to any found in a fast personal computer, and they are equipped to produce graphics that rival those on sophisticated workstations. Add-ons make it possible to use a videogame console to watch DVD movies, send and receive e-mail, and participate in online activities, such as multiplayer games.

- A **mainframe computer** is a large and expensive computer capable of simultaneously processing data for hundreds or thousands of users. Mainframes are generally used by businesses, universities, or governments to provide centralized storage, processing, and management of large amounts of data where reliability, data security, and centralized control are necessary. Its main processing circuitry is housed in a closet-sized cabinet. See Figure A-6.

- A computer is a **supercomputer** if, at the time of construction, it is one of the fastest computers in the world. Because of their speed and complexity, supercomputers can tackle tasks that would not be practical for other computers. Typical uses for supercomputers include breaking codes and modeling worldwide weather systems. A supercomputer CPU is constructed from thousands of microprocessors. As an example, a supercomputer currently under development is designed to use 12,000 microprocessors, which will enable it to operate at speeds exceeding 30 trillion operations per second.

- In the computer industry, the term "server" has several meanings. It can refer to computer hardware, to a specific type of software, or to a combination of hardware and software. In any case, the purpose of a **server** is to "serve" the computers on a network (such as the Internet or a LAN) by supplying them with data. Just about any personal computer, workstation, mainframe, or supercomputer can be configured to perform the work of a server.

FIGURE A-3: A desktop personal computer

▶ A desktop computer fits on a desk and runs on power from an electrical wall outlet; the main unit can be housed in either a vertical case (like the one shown) or a horizontal case

FIGURE A-4: A notebook personal computer

▲ A notebook computer is small and lightweight, giving it the advantage of portability; it can run on power supplied by an electrical outlet, or it can run on battery power

FIGURE A-5: A personal digital assistant

▲ Many handheld computers accept writing input; you can "synchronize" a handheld with a personal computer in order to transfer updated or new information between the two

FIGURE A-6: A mainframe computer

▶ This IBM S/390 mainframe computer weighs about 1,400 lbs. and is about 6.5 feet tall; after additional components are added for storage and output

Examining personal computer systems

The term "**computer system**" usually refers to a computer and all of the input, output, and storage devices that are connected to it. Despite cosmetic differences among personal computers, see Figure A-7, a personal computer system usually includes standard equipment or devices. Devices may vary in color, size, and design for different personal computers. Figure A-8 illustrates a typical desktop personal computer system. Refer to Figure A-8 as you read through the list of devices below.

DETAILS

- **System unit**. The system unit is the case that holds the power supply, storage devices, and the circuit boards, including the main circuit board (also called the "motherboard"), which contains the microprocessor. The system unit for most notebook computers also holds a built-in keyboard and speakers.

- **Monitor**. Most desktop computers use a separate monitor as a display (output) device, whereas notebook computers use a flat panel display screen that is attached to the system unit.

- **Keyboard**. Most computers are equipped with a keyboard as the primary input device.

- **Mouse**. A mouse is a common input device designed to manipulate on-screen graphical objects and controls.

- **Storage devices**. Computers have many types of storage devices that are used to store data when the power is turned off. For example: A **floppy disk drive** is a storage device that reads data from and writes data to floppy disks. A **hard disk drive** can store billions of characters of data. It is usually mounted inside the computer's system unit. A small external light indicates when the drive is in use. A **CD-ROM drive** is a storage device that uses laser technology to read data that is permanently stored on data or audio CDs. A **DVD drive** can read data from data CDs, audio CDs, data DVDs, or DVD movie disks. CD-ROM and DVD drives typically cannot be used to write data onto disks. "ROM" stands for "read-only memory" and means that the drive can read data from disks, but cannot be used to store new data on them. Many computers, especially desktop models, include a **CD-writer** that can be used to create and copy CDs.

- **Speakers** and **sound card**. Desktop computers have a rudimentary built-in speaker that's mostly limited to playing beeps. A small circuit board, called a sound card, is required for high-quality music, narration, and sound effects. A desktop computer's sound card sends signals to external speakers. A notebook's sound card sends signals to speakers that are built into the notebook system unit. The sound card is an input and an output device, while speakers are output devices.

- **Modem**. Virtually every personal computer system includes a built-in modem that can be used to establish an Internet connection using a standard telephone line. A modem is both an input and an output device.

- **Printer**. A computer printer is an output device that produces computer-generated text or graphical images on paper.

What's a peripheral device?

The word "peripheral" dates back to the days of mainframes when the CPU was housed in a giant box, and all input, output, and storage devices were housed separately. Today, the term "peripheral device" designates equipment that might be added to a computer system to enhance its functionality. A printer is a popular peripheral device, as is a digital camera, zip drive, scanner, joystick, or graphics tablet. Though a hard disk drive seems to be an integral part of a computer—after all, it's built right into the system unit—by the strictest technical definition, a hard disk drive would be classified as a peripheral device. The same goes for other storage devices and the keyboard, monitor, LCD screen, sound card, speakers, and modem.

FIGURE A-7: Typical personal computer systems

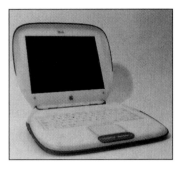

FIGURE A-8: Components of a typical personal computer system

Speakers (sound card is inside the system unit)

Monitor

Printer

Keyboard

Mouse

System unit

CD-ROM drive

CD-writer

Floppy disk drive

Hard disk drive (inside system unit)

Modem (inside system unit)

Exploring data, information, and files

In everyday conversation, people use the terms "data" and "information" interchangeably. Nevertheless, some computer professionals make a distinction between the two terms. They define **data** as the symbols that represent people, events, things, and ideas. Data becomes **information** when it is presented in a format that people can understand and use. As a rule of thumb, remember that data is used by computers; information is used by people. See Figure A-9.

DETAILS

● Have you ever gotten a computer file you couldn't read? It could be because the data has not been converted to information. Computers process and store data using the binary number system and several other codes designed expressly for electronic data. The **binary number system** has only two digits: 0 and 1. The binary number system can represent number data using only 0s and 1s.

● Computers use these codes to store data in a digital format as a series of 1s and 0s. Each 0 or 1 is a **bit**, and 8 bits are called a **byte**. The bits and bytes that are processed and stored by a computer are data. The output results of processing data—the words, numbers, sounds, and graphics—are information.

● A computer stores data in files. A **computer file**, usually referred to simply as a **file**, is a named collection of data that exists on a storage medium, such as a hard disk, a floppy disk, or a CD. Although all files contain data, some files are classified as "data files," whereas other files are classified as "executable files."

● A **data file** contains data. For example, it might contain the text for a document, the numbers for a calculation, the specifications for a graph, the frames of a video, or the notes of a musical passage.

● An **executable file** contains the programs or gives the instructions that tell a computer how to perform a specific task. For example, the word processing program that tells your computer how to display and print text is stored as an executable file.

You can think of data files as passive because the data does not instruct the computer to do anything. Executable files, on the other hand, are active because the instructions stored in the file cause the computer to carry out some action.

● Every file has a name, the **filename**, which often provides a clue to its contents. A file also has a **filename extension** usually referred to simply as an "extension" that further describes a file's contents. For example, in Pbrush.exe, "Pbrush" is the filename and "exe" is the extension. As you can see, the filename is separated from the extension by a period called a "dot." To tell someone the name of this file, you would say, "P brush dot e-x-e."

Executable files typically have .exe extensions. Data files have a variety of extensions, such as .bmp or .tif for a graphic, .mid for synthesized music, or .htm for a Web page. Each software program assigns a specific filename extension to the data files it creates. As a user, you do not decide the extension; rather, it is automatically included when files are created and saved, for example .xls for Excel files or .doc for files created with Word. Depending on your computer settings, you may or may not see the filename extension assigned to a file. Figure A-10 shows a list of files, including the filename extensions.

FIGURE A-9: The difference between data and information

The computer reads the data in the file and produces the output image as information that the viewer can understand

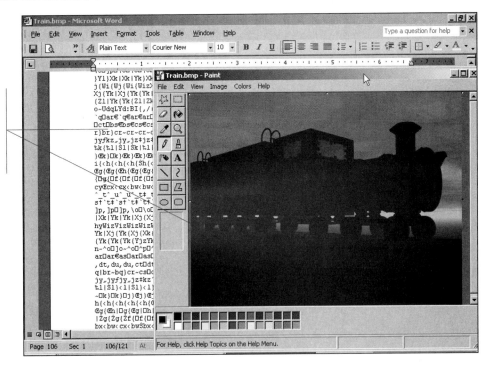

FIGURE A-10: Filenames, including filename extensions

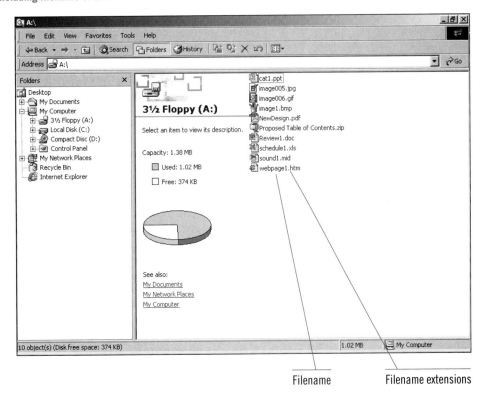

Filename   Filename extensions

UNIT A

Introducing application and system software

A computer's application software and operating system make a computer run. As a computer user, you are probably most familiar with application software. In fact, you probably use many different types of application software that are installed on your computer. As a computer user, your computing experience is driven by the operating system. There is usually only one operating system on your computer; the operating system is not another type of application software. You can run many applications at one time, but only one operating system at one time.

Info Web

APPLE COMPUTERS

DETAILS

- **Application software** is a set of computer programs that helps a person carry out a task. Word processing software, for example, helps people create, edit, and print documents. Personal finance software helps people keep track of their money and investments. Video editing software helps people create and edit home movies and even some professional, commercially-released films.

- An operating system is essentially the master controller for all of the activities that take place within a computer. An **operating system** is classified as **system software**, not application software, because its primary purpose is to help the computer system monitor itself in order to function efficiently. Unlike application software, an operating system does not directly help people perform application-specific tasks, such as word processing. Most of the time people interact with the operating system without realizing it. However, people do interact with the operating system for certain operational and storage tasks, such as starting programs and locating data files.

- Popular personal computer operating systems include Microsoft Windows and Mac OS. Microsoft Windows CE and Palm OS control most handheld computers. Linux and UNIX are popular operating systems for servers. Microsoft Windows (usually referred to simply as "Windows") is probably the most widely used operating system for personal computers. As shown in Figure A-11, the Windows operating system displays menus and simulated on-screen controls designed to be manipulated by a mouse.

- Windows software is not the same as the Windows operating system. The term "Windows software" refers to any application software that is designed to run on computers that use Microsoft Windows as their operating system. For example, a program called Microsoft Word for Windows is a word processing program; it is an application program that is referred to as "Windows software."

- An operating system affects compatibility. Computers that operate in essentially the same way are said to be "compatible." Two of the most important factors that influence compatibility and define a computer's platform are the microprocessor and the operating system. A **platform** consists of the underlying hardware and software of the computer system. Today, two of the most popular personal computer platforms are PCs and Macs. See Figure A-12.

    PCs are based on the design for one of the first personal computer "superstars"—the IBM PC. A huge selection of personal computer brands and models based on the original PC design and manufactured by companies such as IBM, Hewlett-Packard, Toshiba, Dell, and Gateway are on the shelves today. The Windows operating system was designed specifically for these personal computers. Because of this, the PC platform is sometimes called the "Windows platform." Most of the examples in this book pertain to PCs because they are so popular.

    Macs are based on a proprietary design for a personal computer called the Macintosh, manufactured almost exclusively by Apple Computer, Inc. The stylish iMac is one of Apple's most popular computers, and like other computers in the Mac platform, it uses Mac OS as its operating system.

- The PC and Mac platforms are not compatible because their microprocessors and operating systems differ. Consequently, application software designed for Macs does not typically work with PCs. When shopping for new software, it is important to read the package to make sure that it is designed to work with your computer platform.

    Different versions of some operating systems have been created to operate with more than one microprocessor. For example, a version of the Linux operating system exists for the PC platform and another version exists for the Mac platform.

FIGURE A-11: The Windows interface

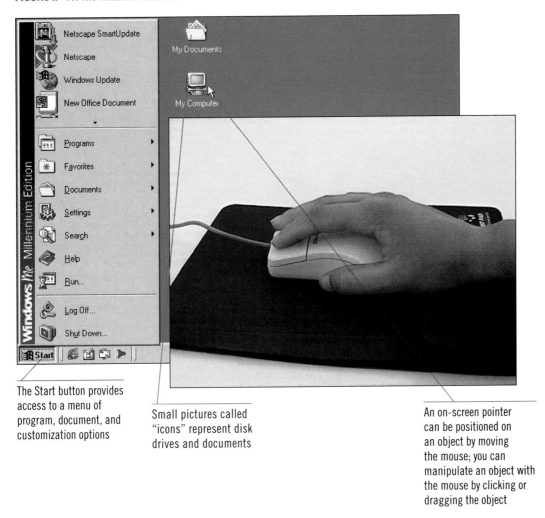

The Start button provides access to a menu of program, document, and customization options

Small pictures called "icons" represent disk drives and documents

An on-screen pointer can be positioned on an object by moving the mouse; you can manipulate an object with the mouse by clicking or dragging the object

FIGURE A-12: The PC and the Mac platforms

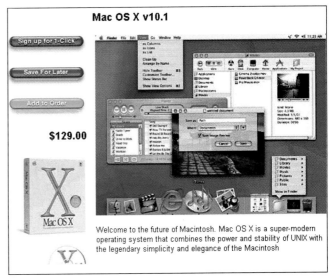

Welcome to the future of Macintosh. Mac OS X is a super-modern operating system that combines the power and stability of UNIX with the legendary simplicity and elegance of the Macintosh

Defining Internet basics

Sometimes referred to as "cyberspace," the **Internet** is a collection of local, regional, national, and international computer networks that are linked together to exchange data and distribute processing tasks. If you're looking for information, if you want to communicate with someone, or if you want to buy something, the Internet offers abundant resources.

DETAILS

- The **Internet backbone** defines the main routes of the Internet. See Figure A-13. Analogous to interstate highways, the Internet backbone is constructed and maintained by major telecommunications companies. These telecommunications links can move huge amounts of data at incredible speeds.

- In addition to the backbone, the Internet encompasses an intricate collection of regional and local communications links. These links can include local telephone systems, cable television lines, cellular telephone systems, and personal satellite dishes that transport data to and from millions of computers and other electronic devices.

- Communication among all of the different devices on the Internet is made possible by **TCP/IP (Transmission Control Protocol/Internet Protocol)**, which is a standard set of rules for electronically addressing and transmitting data.

- Most of the information that is accessible on the Internet is stored on servers. These servers use special **server software** to locate and distribute data requested by Internet users.

- Every device that's connected to the Internet is assigned a unique number, called an **IP address** that pinpoints its location in cyberspace. To prepare data for transport, a computer divides the data into small chunks called **packets**. Each packet is labeled with the IP address of its destination and then transmitted. When a packet reaches an intersection in the Internet's communications links, a device called a **router** examines the packet's address. The router checks the address in a routing table and then sends the packet along the appropriate link towards its destination. As packets arrive at their destinations, they are reassembled into a replica of the original file.

- A **Web site** can provide information, collect information through forms, or provide access to other resources, such as search engines and e-mail.

- The Internet is revolutionizing business by directly linking consumers with retailers, manufacturers, and distributors through electronic commerce, or **E-commerce**. See Figure A-14.

- Electronic mail, known as **e-mail**, allows one person to send an electronic message to another person or to a group of people. A variation of e-mail called a **mailing list server**, or listserv, maintains a public list of people who are interested in a particular topic. Messages sent to the list server are automatically distributed to everyone on the mailing list.

- **Usenet** is a worldwide bulletin board system that contains thousands of discussion forums on every imaginable topic called **newsgroups**. Newsgroup members post messages based on their interests to the bulletin board; these messages can be read and responded to by other group members.

- The Internet allows real-time communication. For example, a **chat group** consists of several people who connect to the Internet and communicate in real time by typing comments to each other. A private version of a chat room, called **instant messaging**, allows people to send typed messages back and forth. **Internet telephony** allows telephone-style conversations to travel over the Internet. Internet telephony requires special software at both ends of the conversation and, instead of a telephone, it uses a microphone connected to a computer.

- The Internet carries radio shows and teleconferences that can be **broadcast** worldwide. Internet radio is popular because broadcasts aren't limited to a small local region.

- Internet servers store a variety of files including documents, music, software, videos, animations, and photos. The process of transferring one of these files from a remote computer, such as a server, to a local computer, such as your personal computer, is called **downloading**. Sending a file from a local computer to a remote computer is called **uploading**. See Figure A-15.

FIGURE A-13: The Internet backbone

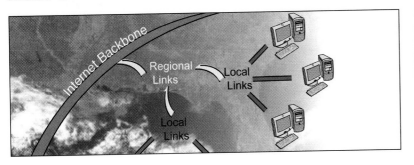

◀ Personal computers are connected to regional and local communications links which in turn connect to the Internet backbone; data transport works seamlessly between any two platforms—between PCs and Macs, and even between personal computers and mainframes

FIGURE A-14: Online auctions

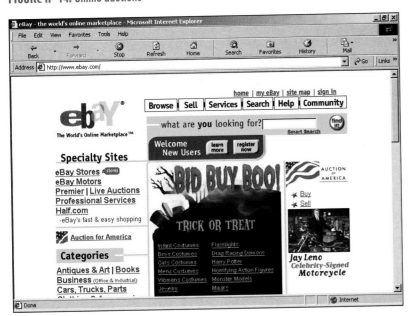

◀ E-commerce includes activities such as online shopping, linking businesses to other businesses (sometimes called e-business or B2B), online stock trading, and electronic auctions

FIGURE A-15: Web sites provide files

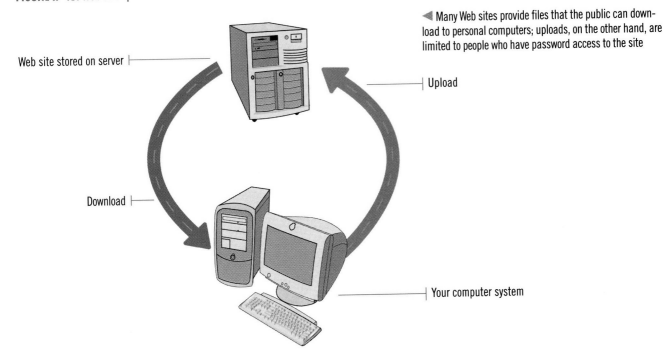

◀ Many Web sites provide files that the public can download to personal computers; uploads, on the other hand, are limited to people who have password access to the site

Connecting to the Internet

To take advantage of the Internet, you'll have to establish a communications link between your computer and the Internet. Possibilities include using your existing telephone line, a cable television line, a personal satellite link, wireless or cell phone service, or special high-speed telephone services. Being on the Internet is often referred to as being **online**.

Info Web

NATIONAL ISPs

DETAILS

● A **dial-up connection** requires a device called a **voice band modem**, or "modem," which converts your computer's digital signals into a type of signal that can travel over telephone lines. Figure A-16 shows various types of computer modems.

To establish a dial-up connection, your computer's modem dials a special access number, which is answered by an Internet modem. Once the connection is established, your computer is "on the Internet." When you complete an Internet session, you must "hang up" your modem. You can choose to disconnect automatically or manually; either way the connection is discontinued until the next time you dial in.

Theoretically, the top speed of a dial-up connection is 56 K, meaning that 56,000 bits of data are transmitted per second. Actual speed is usually reduced by distance, interference, and other technical problems, however, so the speed of most 56 K dial-up connections is more like 45 K. This speed is useable for e-mail, e-commerce, and chat. It is not, however, really optimal for applications that require large amounts of data to be transferred quickly over the Internet.

● **Cable modem service** is offered to a cable company's customers for an additional monthly charge and usually requires two pieces of equipment: a network card and a cable modem. A **network card** is a device that's designed to connect a personal computer to a local area network. A **cable modem** is a device that changes a computer's signals into a form that can travel over cable TV links.

Cable modem access is referred to as an **always-on connection**, because your computer is, in effect, always connected to the Internet, unlike a dial-up connection that is established only when the dialing sequence is completed. A cable modem receives data more than 25 times faster than a dial-up connection. This speed is suitable for most Internet activities, including real-time video and teleconferencing.

● Many telephone and independent telecommunications companies offer high-speed, always-on connections. **ISDN (Integrated Services Digital Network)** provides data transfer speeds of either 64 K (bits per second, or bps) or 128 K (bps). Given data transfer speeds that are only marginally better than a 56 K dial-up

connection and substantial monthly fees, ISDN ranks low on the list of high-speed Internet options for most consumers. **DSL (Digital Subscriber Line)** and **xDSL** are generic names for a family of high-speed Internet links, including ADSL, SDSL, and DSL lite. Each type of DSL provides different maximum speeds from twice as fast to approximately 125 times faster than a 56 K dial-up connection. Both ISDN and DSL connections require proximity to a telephone switching station, which can be a problem for speed-hungry consumers who don't live near one.

● Another Internet connection option is **DSS (Digital Satellite Service)**, which today offers two-way Internet access at an average speed of about 500 K. Consumers are required to rent or purchase a satellite dish and pay for its installation.

● An **ISP (Internet Service Provider)** is a company that maintains Internet computers and telecommunications equipment in order to provide Internet access to businesses, organizations, and individuals. Some parts of the Internet (such as military computers) are off limits to the general public. Other parts of the Internet (such as the New York Times archives) limit access to paid members. Many parts of the Internet encourage memberships and offer additional perks if you sign up.

● User IDs and passwords are designed to provide access to authorized users and to prevent unauthorized access. A **user ID** is a series of characters, letters, and possibly numbers that becomes a person's unique identifier, similar to a social security number. A **password** is a different series of characters that verifies the user ID, sort of like a PIN (personal identification number) verifies your identity at an ATM machine.

● Typically, your ISP provides you with a user ID and password that you use to connect to the Internet. You will accumulate additional user IDs and passwords from other sources for specific Internet activities, such as reading New York Times articles, or participating in an online auction. The process of entering a user ID and password is usually referred to as "logging in" or "logging on." See Figure A-17. The rules for creating a user ID are not consistent throughout the Internet, so it is important to read all of the instructions carefully before finalizing your ID.

FIGURE A-16: Computer modems

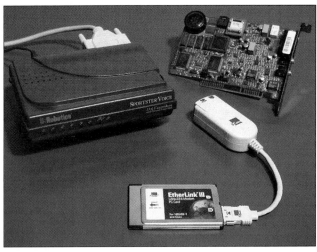

▲ To determine whether a computer has a modem, look for a place to plug in a standard phone cable

▲ An external modem (top left) connects to the computer with a cable; an internal modem (top right) is installed inside the computer's system unit; a PC card modem (bottom center) is typically used in a notebook computer

▲ A modem card slides into a notebook computer's PC card slot

FIGURE A-17: Entering a password

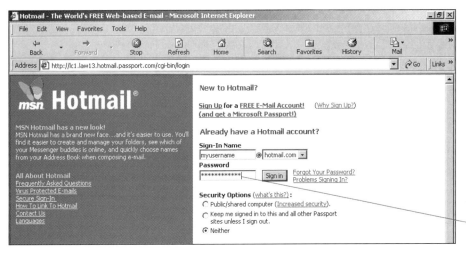

◄ Don't share your password with anyone, or write it down where it could be found; your password should be a sequence of characters and numbers that is easy for you to remember, but would be difficult for someone else to guess

Typically, when you log in and enter your password, a series of asterisks appears on the screen

What service does an Internet service provider provide?

To access the Internet, you do not typically connect your computer directly to the backbone. Instead, you connect it to an ISP that in turn connects to the backbone. An ISP is a point of access to the Internet. An ISP typically provides a connection to the Internet and an e-mail account. ISP customers arrange for service, in this case for Internet access, for which they pay a monthly fee. In addition to a monthly fee, an ISP might also charge an installation fee. In Europe, subscribers may also be required to pay per-minute fees, similar to cell phone charges. The ISP that you select should provide service in the places that you typically use your computer. If your work takes you on the road a lot, you'll want to consider a national ISP that provides local access numbers in the cities that you visit. An ISP usually specializes in one type of service. The quality of dial-up and cable modem services tends to decrease as the number of customers increases due to increased traffic.

Understanding World Wide Web basics

In the 1960s, long before personal computers or the Internet existed, a Harvard student named Ted Nelson wrote a term paper in which he described a set of documents, called **hypertext**, that would be stored on a computer. While reading a document in hypertext, a person could use a set of "links" to view related documents. A revolutionary idea for its time, today hypertext is the foundation for a part of the Internet that's often called "the Web" by the millions of people who use it every day.

Info Web
HYPERTEXT

DETAILS

- One of the Internet's most captivating attractions, the **Web** (short for "World Wide Web") is a collection of files that are interconnected through the use of hypertext. Many of these files produce documents called **Web pages**. Other files contain photos, videos, animations, and sounds that can be incorporated into specific Web pages. Most Web pages contain **links** (sometimes called "hyperlinks") to related documents and media files. See Figure A-18.

- A series of Web pages can be grouped into a **Web site**—a sort of virtual "place" in cyberspace. Every day, thousands of people shop at online department stores featuring clothing, shoes, and jewelry; visit research Web sites to look up information; and go to news Web sites, not only to read about the latest news, sports, and weather, but also to discuss current issues with other readers. The Web encompasses these and many other types of sites.

- Web sites are hosted by corporations, government agencies, colleges, and private organizations all over the world. The computers and software that store and distribute Web pages are called **Web servers**.

- Every Web page has a unique address called a **URL (uniform resource locator)**. For example, the URL for the Cable News Network Web site is http://www.cnn.com. Most URLs begin with http://. **HTTP (Hypertext Transfer Protocol)** is the communications standard that's instrumental in ferrying Web documents to all corners of the Internet. When typing a URL, the http:// can usually be omitted, so www.cnn.com works just as well as http://www.cnn.com.

- Most Web sites have a main page that acts as a doorway to the rest of the pages at the site. This main page is sometimes referred to as a **home page**. The URL for a Web site's main page is typically short and to the point, like www.cnn.com.

  The site might then be divided into topic areas that are reflected in the URL. For example, the CNN site might include a weather center www.cnn.com/weather/ and an entertainment desk www.cnn.com/showbiz/. A series of Web pages will then be grouped under the appropriate topic. For example, you might find a page about hurricanes at the URL www.cnn.com/weather/hurricanes.html or a page about el niño at www.cnn.com/weather/elnino.htm. The filename of a specific Web page always appears last in the URL—hurricanes.html and elnino.htm are the names of two Web pages. Web page filenames usually have an .htm or .html extension, indicating that the page was created with **HTML** (Hyptertext Markup Language), a standard format for Web documents. Figure A-19 identifies the parts of a URL.

- A URL never contains a space, even after a punctuation mark. An underline character is sometimes used to give the appearance of a space between words, as in the URL www.detroit.com/restaurants/best_restaurants.html. Be sure to use the correct type of slash—always a forward slash (/)—and duplicate the URL's capitalization exactly. The servers that run some Web sites are case sensitive, which means that an uppercase letter is not the same as a lowercase letter. On these servers, typing www.cmu.edu/Overview.html (with an uppercase "O") will not locate the page that's stored as www.cmu.edu/overview.html (with a lowercase "o").

FIGURE A-18: A Web page

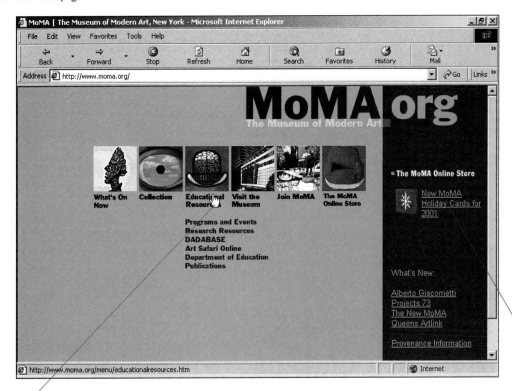

To determine whether an object is a link, position the pointer on it; if the pointer changes to a hand shape, the object is a link; to activate a link, simply click it

On most Web pages, underlined text indicates a link

FIGURE A-19: A URL

http://www.cnn.com/showbiz/movies.htm

| Web protocol standard | Web server name | Folder name | Document name and filename extension |

◄ The URL for a Web page indicates the computer on which it is stored, its location on the Web server, a folder name, its filename, and its filename extension

Using browsers

A Web browser, usually referred to simply as a **browser**, is a software program that runs on your computer and helps you access Web pages. A browser fetches and displays Web pages. Two of today's most popular browsers are Microsoft Internet Explorer® (IE) and Netscape Navigator® (Navigator). Browser software provides a set of tools for viewing and navigating Web pages.

DETAILS

- Whether it's called a "URL box," an "Address box," a "Location box," or a "Netsite box," most browsers provide a space for entering URLs.

- If you want to view the Web page located at www.dogs.com/boxer.html, you enter the URL into the Address box provided by your browser. When you press [Enter] on the keyboard, the browser contacts the Web server at www.dogs.com and requests the boxer.html page. The server sends your computer the data stored in boxer.html. This data includes two things: the information that you want to view and embedded codes, called **HTML tags**, that tell your browser how to display the information. The tags specify details such as the color of the background, the text color and size, and the placement of graphics. Figure A-20, which shows a page in Internet Explorer and the HTML code used to display the page, shows that a browser assembles a document on your computer screen according to the specifications contained in the HTML tags.

- Web browsers offer a remarkably similar set of features and capabilities. HTML tags make it possible for Web pages to appear similar from one browser to the next.

- After you look at a sequence of pages, the browser's Back button lets you retrace your steps to view pages that you've seen previously. Most browsers also have a Forward button, which shows you the page that you were viewing before you pressed the Back button.

- Your browser lets you select a **home page**, which is the Web page that appears every time you start your browser. The idea is that you'll select a home page that contains links or information

that you use often. Whenever you click the Home button, your browser displays your home page. This home page is different than the home page of a Web site which was defined earlier.

- Typically, a browser provides access to a print option from a button or a menu, allowing you to print the contents of a Web page. You should always preview before printing because a Web page on the screen may print out as several printed pages. Most browsers let you save a copy of a Web page and place it at the storage location of your choice, and allow you to save a copy of a graphic or sound that you find on a Web page. Most browsers also provide a Copy command that allows you to copy a section of text from a Web page, which you can then paste into one of your own documents. To keep track of the source for each insertion, you can also use the Copy command to copy the Web page's URL from the Address box and then paste the URL into your document.

- To help you revisit sites from previous sessions, your browser provides a **History list**. You can display this list by clicking a button or menu option provided by your browser. To revisit any site in the History list, click its URL. Many browsers allow you to specify how long a URL will remain in the History list.

- If you find a great Web site and you want to revisit it sometime in the future, you can add the URL to a list, typically called **Favorites** or **Bookmarks** so you can simply click its URL to display it.

- Sometimes a Web page takes a very long time to appear on your screen. If you don't want to wait for a page, click the Stop button.

- If you're looking for specific information on a "long" Web page, you can save yourself a lot of reading by using the Find option on your browser's Edit menu to locate a particular word or phrase.

Using search engines

The term "**search engine**" popularly refers to a Web site that provides a variety of tools to help you find information on the Web. A **keyword** is any word or phrase that you type to describe the information that you're trying to find. Based on your input, the search engine provides a list of pages. Depending on the search engine that you use, you may be able to find information by entering a description, filling out a form, or clicking a series of links to review a list of topics and subtopics (Topic Directory). See Figure A-21. Without search engines, using the Internet would be like trying to find a book in the Library of Congress by wandering around the stacks. To discover exactly how to use a particular search engine effectively, refer to its Help pages.

FIGURE A-20: Internet Explorer browser

```
<HTML>
<HEAD><TITLE>From the North Woods</TITLE></HEAD>
<BODY>
<CENTER>
<FONT SIZE=+3>North Woods Update</FONT><BR>
<B>Brought to you by Frank Parker, Forestry Student</B>
</CENTER>
<BR>
<OL>
<LI> Never place your tongue on frozen  metal.
<LI> Always take your boots off in the sauna.
</OL>
<HR>
<IMG SRC="Chevy.jpg
Today's Feature:
<A HREF = "parker/€
Chevrolet </A>
</BODY>
<HTML>
```

An HTML document is basically a running string of text with embedded HTML tags, such as this tag that instructs the browser to center a line of text

When the browser displays the Web page, the specified text is centered

A browser provides a sort of window in which it displays a Web page; the border of the window contains a set of menus and controls to help you navigate from one Web page to another

A browser uses HTML tags embedded in a document to correctly display text, titles, colors, links, and graphics

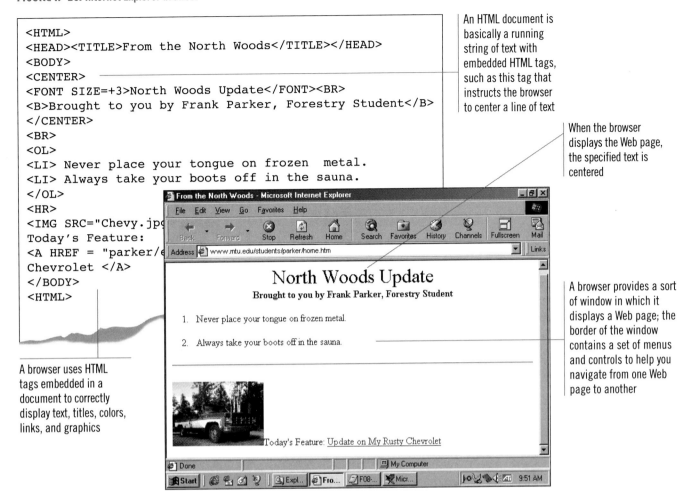

FIGURE A-21: Search engines

The search was for railroad cars

The search engine displays the total number of relevant pages

Underlined links make it easy to quickly connect to any of the Web pages in the list

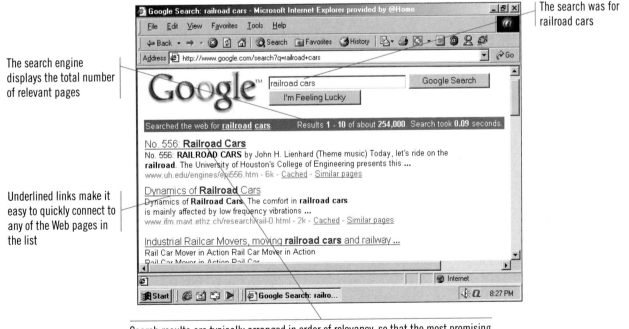

Search results are typically arranged in order of relevancy, so that the most promising Web pages should be at the top of the list; a brief description of the page helps you determine whether you want to view it

Understanding e-mail basics

The Internet really took off when people discovered electronic mail. Billions of e-mail messages speed over the Internet each year. E-mail can refer to a single electronic message or to the entire system of computers and software that transmits, receives, and stores e-mail messages. Any person with an e-mail account can send and receive e-mail.

DETAILS

- An **e-mail account** provides the rights to a storage area, or mailbox, supplied by an e-mail provider, such as an ISP. Each mailbox has a unique address that typically consists of a user ID, an @ symbol, and the name of the computer that maintains the mailbox. For example, suppose that a university student named Dee Greene has an electronic mailbox on a computer called rutgers.edu. If her user ID is "dee_greene," her **e-mail address** would be dee_greene@rutgers.edu.

- An **e-mail message** is a document that is composed on a computer and transmitted in digital or "electronic" form to another computer. Every message includes a message header and the body of the message, usually displayed in a form, as shown in Figure A-22. Basic e-mail activities include writing, reading, replying to, and forwarding messages. Messages can be printed, kept for later reference, or deleted.

- Any file that travels with an e-mail message is called an **e-mail attachment**.

- After you receive an e-mail message, you can use the Forward feature to pass it on to other people. When you initiate the forward process, the original e-mail message is copied into a new message window, complete with the address of the original sender. You can then enter the address of the person to whom you are forwarding the message. You can also add a note about why you are passing the message along.

- By default, e-mail messages are stored in a simple format called ASCII text. No fancy formatting is allowed, no variation in font type or color, no underlining or boldface, and of course, no pictures or sounds.

- Today, most e-mail software allows you to create e-mail messages in HTML format. Why use HTML format for your mail? HTML messages can contain fancy formatting. The only limitation is that your e-mail recipients must have HTML-compliant e-mail software; otherwise, your message will be delivered as plain old ASCII text.

- Although e-mail is delivered quickly, it is important to use proper netiquette when composing a message. **Netiquette** (Internet etiquette) is a series of customs or guidelines for maintaining civilized and effective communications in online discussions and e-mail exchanges. For example, typing in all caps, such as "WHAT DID YOU DO?" is considered shouting and rude.

- An **e-mail system** is the equipment and software that carries and manipulates e-mail messages. It includes computers and software called **e-mail servers** that sort, store, and route mail.

- E-mail is based on **store-and-forward technology**, a communications method in which data that cannot be sent directly to its destination will be temporarily stored until transmission is possible. This technology allows e-mail messages to be routed to a server and held until they are forwarded to the next server or to a personal mailbox.

- Three types of e-mail systems are widely used today: POP, IMAP, and Web-based mail. **POP (Post Office Protocol)** temporarily stores new messages in your mailbox on an e-mail server. See Figure A-23. Most people who use POP have obtained an e-mail account from an ISP. Such an account provides a mailbox on the ISP's **POP server**, which is a computer that stores your incoming messages until they can be transferred to your hard disk. Using POP requires e-mail client software. This software, which is installed on your computer, provides an Inbox and an Outbox. When you ask the e-mail server to deliver your mail, all of the messages stored in your mailbox on the POP server are transferred to your computer, stored on your computer's disk drive, and listed as new mail in your Inbox. You can then disconnect from the Internet, if you like, and read the new mail at your leisure.

  IMAP (Internet Messaging Access Protocol) is similar to POP, except that you have the option of downloading your mail or leaving it on the server. **Web-based e-mail**, the most commonly used, keeps your mail at a Web site rather than transferring it to your computer. Examples of Web-based e-mail are Yahoo mail and Hotmail. Before you can use Web-based e-mail, you'll need an e-mail account with a Web-based e-mail provider.

FIGURE A-22: Composing an e-mail message

When you compose an e-mail message, you'll begin by entering the address of one or more recipients and the subject of the message

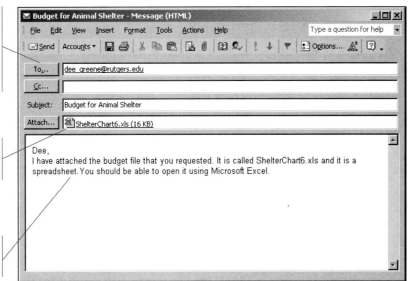

When the message is sent, your e-mail software adds the date and your e-mail address to identify you as the sender

You can also specify one or more files to attach to the message

The body of the e-mail message contains the message itself

FIGURE A-23: Incoming and outgoing mail

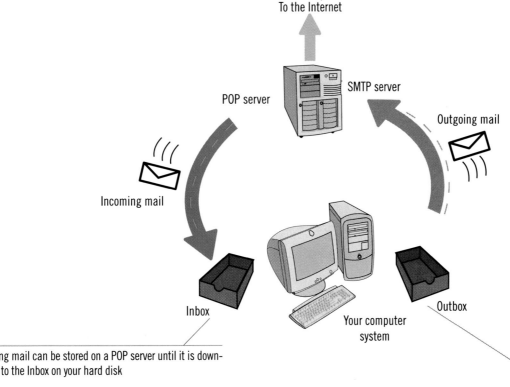

To the Internet

POP server

SMTP server

Outgoing mail

Incoming mail

When you go online, you can send all the mail that's being held in your Outbox; outgoing mail is routed by an SMTP (Simple Mail Transfer Protocol) server, instead of by the POP server

Inbox

Your computer system

Outbox

Incoming mail can be stored on a POP server until it is downloaded to the Inbox on your hard disk

An Outbox temporarily holds mesages that you composed and completed, but that haven't been transmitted over the Internet

The Boot Process

The sequence of events that occurs between the time that you turn on a computer and the time that it becomes ready to accept commands is referred to as the **boot process** or "booting" your computer. Your computer boots up by first loading a small program, called a "bootstrap" program, into memory, then it uses that small program to load a large operating system. Your computer's small bootstrap program is built into special ROM (read-only memory) circuitry housed in the computer's system unit. When you turn on a computer, the ROM circuitry receives power and it begins the boot process.

What is the purpose of the boot process? The boot process involves a lot of flashing lights, whirring noises, and beeping as your computer performs a set of diagnostic tests called the **power-on self-test (POST)**. The good news is that these tests can warn you if certain crucial components of your computer system are out of whack. The bad news is that these tests cannot warn you of impending failures. Also, problems identified during the boot process usually must be fixed before you can start a computing session.

The boot process serves an additional purpose—loading the operating system from the hard disk and into memory so that it can help the computer carry out basic operations. Without the operating system, a computer's CPU is basically unable to communicate with any input, output, or storage devices. It can't display information, accept commands, store data, or run any application software. Therefore, loading the operating system is a crucial step in the boot process.

Most of a computer's memory is "volatile" random access memory (RAM), which cannot hold any data when the power is off. Although a copy of the operating system is housed in RAM while the computer is in operation, this copy is erased as soon as the power is turned off. Given the volatility of RAM, computer designers decided to store the operating system on a computer's hard disk. During the boot process, a copy of the operating system is copied into RAM, where it can be accessed quickly whenever the computer needs to carry out an input, output, or storage operation. The operating system remains in RAM until the computer is turned off.

Six major events happen during the boot process:

1. Power up. When you turn on the power switch, the power light is illuminated, and power is distributed to the computer circuitry.

2. Start boot program. The microprocessor begins to execute the bootstrap program that is stored in ROM.

3. Power-on self-test. The computer performs diagnostic tests of several crucial system components.

4. Identify peripheral devices. The operating system identifies the peripheral devices that are connected to a computer and checks their settings.

5. Load operating system. The operating system is copied from the hard disk to RAM.

6. Check configuration and customization. The microprocessor reads configuration data and executes any customized startup routines specified by the user.

What if I turn on a computer and nothing happens? The first step in the boot process is the power-up stage. Power from a wall outlet or battery activates a small power light. If the power light does not come on when you flip the "on" switch, you should check all the power connections and be sure everything is plugged in properly.

What kinds of problems are likely to show up during the power-on self-test? The POST checks your computer's main circuitry, screen display, memory, and keyboard. It can identify when one of these devices has failed, but it cannot identify intermittent problems or impending failures. The POST notifies you of a hardware problem by displaying an error message on the screen or by emitting a series of beeps. A **beep code** provides your computer with a way to signal a problem, even if the screen is not functioning. You can check the documentation or Web site for your computer to find the specific meaning of numeric error codes. The printed or online reference manual for a computer usually explains the meaning of each beep code.

Should I try to fix these problems myself? If a computer displays error messages, emits beep codes, or seems to freeze up during the boot process, you can take some simple steps that might fix it. First, turn the computer off, check all the cables, wait five seconds, then try to start the computer again. Refer to Figure A-24 for a power-up checklist. If you still encounter a boot error after trying to restart the computer several times, contact a technical support person.

What's the long list of stuff that appears on my screen during the boot process? After the POST, the bootstrap program tries to identify all of the devices that are connected to the computer. The settings for each device appear on the screen, creating a list of rather esoteric information.

On occasion, a device gets skipped or misidentified during the boot process. An error message is not produced, but the device doesn't seem to work properly. To resolve this problem, shut down the computer and reboot it. If a device is causing persistent problems, you may need to check the manufacturer's Web site to see if a new software patch will improve its operation.

Do computers have trouble loading the operating system or applying customization settings? Problems during the last stages of the boot process are rare, except when a disk has been inadvertently left in the floppy disk drive. Before computers were equipped with hard disk drives, floppy disks were used to store the operating system and application software. As a legacy from these early machines, today's computers first check the floppy disk drive for a disk containing the operating system. If it doesn't find a disk in the drive, it proceeds to look for the operating system on the hard disk. However, if a floppy disk happens to be left in drive A, the computer will assume that you want to boot from it and will look for the operating system on that disk. The error message "Non-system disk or disk error" is the clue to this problem. Remove the floppy disk and press any key to resume the boot process.

How do I know when the boot process is finished? The boot process is complete when the computer is ready to accept your commands. Usually, the computer displays an operating system prompt or main screen. The Windows operating system, for example, displays the Windows desktop when the boot process is complete.

If Windows cannot complete the boot process, you are likely to see a menu that contains an option for Safe Mode. **Safe Mode** is a limited version of Windows that allows you to use your mouse, monitor, and keyboard, but not other peripheral devices. This mode is designed for troubleshooting, not for real computing tasks. If your computer enters Safe Mode at the end of the boot process, you should use the Shut Down command on the Start menu to shut down and turn off your computer properly. You can then turn on your computer again. It should complete the boot process in regular Windows mode. If your computer enters Safe Mode again, consult a technician.

FIGURE A-24: Power-Up checklist

☑	Make sure that the power cable is plugged into the wall and into the back of the computer.
☑	Check batteries if you're using a notebook computer.
☑	Try to plug your notebook into a wall outlet.
☑	Make sure that the wall outlet is supplying power (plug a lamp into it and make sure that you can turn it on).
☑	If the computer is plugged into a surge strip, extension cord, or uninterruptible power supply, make sure that it is turned on and functioning correctly.
☑	Can you hear the fan in your desktop computer? If not, the computer's power supply mechanism might have failed.

How Private is E-mail?

When you drop an envelope in the corner mailbox, you probably expect it to arrive at its destination unopened, and with its contents kept safe from prying eyes. When you make a phone call, you might assume that your conversation will proceed unmonitored by wiretaps or other listening devices. Can you also expect an e-mail message to be read only by the person to whom it is addressed?

In the U.S., The Electronic Communications Privacy Act of 2000 prohibits the use of intercepted e-mail as evidence unless a judge approved a search warrant. That doesn't mean, however, that the government can't or isn't reading your mail. The FBI developed a technology called Carnivore that scans through messages entering and leaving an ISP's e-mail system and looks for e-mail associated with a person who is under investigation. Privacy advocates are concerned because Carnivore scans all of the messages that pass through an ISP, not just those messages destined for a particular individual.

Law enforcement agencies are required to obtain a search warrant before intercepting e-mail. No such restriction, however, exists for employers who want to monitor employee e-mail. According to the American Management Association, 27 percent of U.S. businesses monitor employee e-mail. But this intentional eavesdropping is only one way in which the contents of your e-mail messages might become public. The recipient of your e-mail can forward it to one or more people, people you never intended to read it. Your e-mail messages can pop up on a technician's screen in the course of system maintenance or repairs. Also, keep in mind that e-mail messages, including those that you delete from your own PC, can be stored on backups of your ISP's e-mail server.

The United States Omnibus Crime Control and Safe Streets Act of 1968 and the Electronic Communications Privacy Act of 1986 prohibit public and private employers from engaging in surreptitious surveillance of employee activity through the use of electronic devices. However, two exceptions to these privacy statutes exist. The first exception permits an employer to monitor e-mail if one party to the communication consents to the monitoring. An employer must inform employees of this policy before undertaking any monitoring. The second exception permits employers to monitor their employees' e-mail if a legitimate business need exists and the monitoring takes place within the business-owned e-mail system.

Employees have not been successful in defending their rights to e-mail privacy. For example, in 1996, a Pillsbury employee was fired from his job for making unprofessional comments in an e-mail to his supervisor. Like employees of a business, students who use a school's e-mail system cannot be assured of e-mail privacy. When a CalTech student was accused of sexually harassing a female student by sending lewd e-mail to her and her boyfriend, investigators retrieved all of the student's e-mail from the archives of the e-mail server. The student was expelled from the university even though he claimed that the e-mail had been "spoofed" to make it look as though he had sent it, when it had actually been sent by someone else.

Why would an employer want to know the contents of employee e-mail? Why would a school be concerned with the correspondence of its students? An organization that owns an e-mail system can be held responsible for the consequences of actions related to the contents of e-mail messages on that system.

Many schools and businesses have established e-mail privacy policies that explain the conditions under which you can and cannot expect your e-mail to remain private. Court decisions, however, seem to support the notion that because an organization owns and operates its e-mail system, the organization owns the e-mail messages that are generated on its system. The individual who authors an e-mail message does not own it and therefore has no rights related to it. A company can therefore legally monitor your e-mail.

You should use your e-mail account with the expectation that some of your mail will be read from time to time. Think of your e-mail as a postcard, rather than a letter, and save your controversial comments for face-to-face conversations.

▼ EXPAND THE IDEAS

1. How private do you think your e-mail is? Discuss in class. Support your ideas with concrete examples.

2. Would you have different privacy expectations regarding an e-mail account at your place of work than you would for an account that you purchase from an e-mail service provider? Write a short paper in which you present your opinions.

3. Do you agree that a college should be able to expel a student accused of sending harassing e-mail to another student? Research cases where this might have occurred. Write a short paper that details at least one recent case. Include at least one paragraph presenting your view on the issue: whether or not you agree with the outcome of the case. Be sure to include your sources.

Issue

End of Unit Exercises

▼ KEY TERMS

Always-on connection	E-mail account	ISDN	Power-on self-test (POST)
Application software	E-mail address	ISP	Printer
Beep code	E-mail attachment	Keyboard	Processing
Binary number system	E-mail message	Keyword	Router
Bit	E-mail servers	LAN (Local area network)	Safe Mode
Bookmarks	E-mail system	Links	Search engine
Boot process	Executable file	Macs	Server
Browser	Favorites	Mailing list server	Server software
Byte	File	Mainframe computer	Software
Cable modem	Filename	Memory	Sound card
Cable modem service	Filename extension	Microcomputer	Speakers
CD-ROM drive	Floppy disk drive	Microprocessor	Storage
CD-writer	Handheld computer	Modem	Store-and-forward technology
Central processing unit (CPU)	Hard disk drive	Monitor	Stored program
Chat group	Hardware	Mouse	Supercomputer
Computer	History list	Netiquette	System software
Computer file	Home page	Network card	System unit
Computer network	HTML	Newsgroups	TCP/IP
Computer program	HTML tags	Notebook computer	Uploading
Computer system	HTTP	Online	URL
Data	Hypertext	Operating system	Usenet
Data file	IMAP	Output	User ID
Desktop computer	Information	Output device	Videogame console
Dial-up connection	Input	Password	Voice band modem
Downloading	Input device	PDA	Web
DSL	Instant messaging	Peripheral device	Web pages
DSS	Internet	Personal computer (PC)	Web servers
DVD drive	Internet backbone	Platform	Web site
E-commerce	Internet telephony	POP	Web-based e-mail
E-mail	IP address	POP server	Workstation

▼ UNIT REVIEW

1. Make sure that you can define each of the key terms in this unit in your own words. Select 10 of the terms with which you are unfamiliar and write a sentence for each of them.

2. Explain the basic functions of a computer: inputting, processing, storing, and outputting. Explain why the stored program concept is important to all of this.

3. Identify and describe each of the components of a basic personal computer system.

4. Describe the difference between an operating system and application software.

5. Define computer platform. Then discuss what makes two computer platforms compatible or incompatible.

6. List at least five resources that are provided by the Internet and identify those that are most popular.

7. Make a list of the ways to connect to the Internet presented in this unit and specify characteristics of each.

8. Describe the components of a URL and of an e-mail address.

9. Make a list of the rules that you should follow when typing a URL.

10. Define "browser," then describe how a browser helps you navigate the Web.

▼ FILL IN THE BEST ANSWER

1. The basic functions of a computer are to accept _____, process data, store data, and produce output.

2. A computer processes data in the _____ processing unit.

3. The idea of a(n) _____ program means that instructions for a computing task can be loaded into a computer's memory.

4. The _____ unit is the case that holds the main circuit boards, microprocessor, power supply, and storage devices for a personal computer system.

5. A device that is an integral part of a computer but that can be added to a computer is called a(n) _____ device.

6. Executable files usually have a(n) _____ extension.

7. A(n) _____ system is the software that acts as the master controller for all of the activities that take place within a computer system.

8. The main routes of the Internet are referred to as the Internet _____.

9. Communication between all of the different devices on the Internet is made possible by _____ /IP.

10. Most of the "stuff" that's accessible on the Internet is stored on _____ that are maintained by various businesses and organizations.

11. A dial-up connection requires a device called a(n) _____ band modem.

12. To use a cable Internet connection you need a cable modem and a(n) _____.

13. A cable modem provides an always _____ connection to the Internet.

14. The process of entering a user ID and password is referred to as _____.

15. Every Web page has a unique address called a(n) _____.

16. A browser assembles a Web page on your computer screen according to the specifications contained in the _____ tags.

17. Whenever you start your browser, it displays your _____ page.

18. A(n) _____ fetches and displays Web pages.

19. Store-and-forward technology stores messages on an e-mail _____ until they are forwarded to an individual's computer.

20. For many e-mail systems, a(n) _____ server handles incoming mail, and a(n) _____ server handles outgoing mail.

▼ INDEPENDENT CHALLENGE 1

When discussing computers and computer concepts it is important to use proper terminology. Unit A presented you with many computer terms that describe computer equipment. If you would like to explore any of the terms in more detail, there are online dictionaries that can help you expand your understanding of these terms.

1. For this independent challenge, write a one-page paper that describes the computer that you use most frequently.

2. Refer to the Key Terms used in this unit and use terms from this unit to describe your computer components and the functions they perform.

3. In your final draft, underline each Key Term that you used in your paper. Follow your professor's instructions for submitting your paper as an e-mail attachment or as a printed document.

▼ INDEPENDENT CHALLENGE 2

Suppose that producers for a television game show ask you to help them create a set of computer-related questions for the next show. You will compose a set of 10 questions based on the information provided in Unit A. Each question should be in multiple-choice format with four possible answers.

1. Write 10 questions: two very simple questions, five questions of medium difficulty, and three difficult questions. Each question should be on an index card.

2. For each question, indicate the correct answer on the back of each card and the page in this book on which the answer can be found.

3. Gather in small groups and take turns asking each other the questions.

▼ INDEPENDENT CHALLENGE 3

 The Issue section of this unit focused on how much (or how little) privacy you can expect when using an e-mail account. For this independent challenge, you will write a two- to five-page paper about e-mail privacy based on information that you gather from the Internet.

1. To begin this Independent Challenge, consult the E-mail Privacy InfoWeb and link to the recommended Web pages to get an in-depth overview of the issue.

2. Determine the viewpoint that you will present in your paper about e-mail privacy. You might, for example, decide to present the viewpoint of a student who believes that e-mail should be afforded the same privacy rights as a sealed letter. Or you might present the viewpoint of an employer who wants to explain why your business believes that it is necessary to monitor employee e-mail. Whatever viewpoint you decide to present, make sure that you can back it up with facts and references to authoritative articles and Web pages.

3. Place citations to your research (include the author's name, article title, date of publication, and URL) at the end of your paper as endnotes, on each page as footnotes, or along with the appropriate paragraphs using parentheses. Follow your professor's instructions for submitting your paper via e-mail or as a printed document.

▼ INDEPENDENT CHALLENGE 4

 A new ISP is getting ready to open in your area, and the president of the company asks you to design a print ad. Your ad must communicate all pertinent information about the ISP.

1. Before starting on the design, use your favorite search engine to find out more about ISPs in your area. Gather information to use in your ad, such as the type of services offered (dial-up, cable modem, etc.), the speed of service, the geographical coverage, price, and special or proprietary services.

2. Make up a name for your ISP. Design a print ad for the company using a computer or freehand tools. Submit your ad design along with a short written summary that describes how this ad reflects the ISP and the services it offers.

▼ VISUAL WORKSHOP

The digital divide is defined as the difference in rates of access to computers and the Internet among different demographic groups. With the explosion of the Internet and the technology that drives the information age, forward-thinking social reformers recognized early on the potential for a divide between the "haves" and the "have nots." Not-for-profit organizations, concerned with the impact of the digital divide, designed studies to help them analyze the causes and effects of this phenomenon. These studies have been conducted for the past few decades.

FIGURE A-25

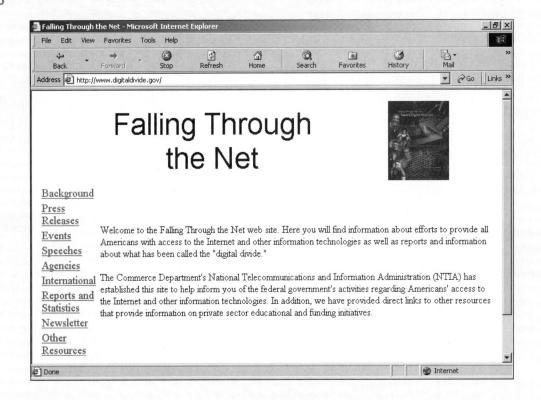

1. Is there a solution to the digital divide? Connect to the Internet and use your favorite search engine to search on the key phrase "digital divide." Among the sites you should find is the Digital Divide Web site at www.digitaldivide.gov, which is shown in Figure A-25. This site includes links to articles and research studies that address the digital divide. Review the findings for two studies or articles. Write a short paper summarizing these studies or articles. In your conclusion, comment on how you feel the digital divide affects our society and what we as a society should do about it, if anything.

2. Could you live without computers? Computers are ubiquitous; beyond the obvious applications, such as using your word processor to write a report, you come in contact with them during the course of your day in simple activities such as shopping in a supermarket or getting cash from your bank's ATM machine. Create a log to track your daily activities that involve computers. Keep the log for one week. At the end of the week, write a summary of any surprises or insights you have as to how computers affect your life.

3. Is there a digital divide in your community? Create a survey that will determine Internet access and computer ownership among people that you know. The survey should consist of 5-10 questions. You want to find out, within a chosen sector, who owns a computer, if they own more than one, what they use the computer(s) for, if they have Internet access, and if they access the Internet from their home or elsewhere. Be sure to survey at least 20 people. The survey should be anonymous but include demographic information. Compile the results of your survey into a chart and write a short summary explaining your findings.

UNIT B

Computer Hardware

OBJECTIVES

Introduce storage technology
Compare storage technologies
Compare storage media and devices
Explore floppy disk technology
Explore hard disk technology
Explore CD/DVD technology
Understand expansion slots, cards, ports, and cables
Compare display devices
Compare printers
Examine keyboards
Explore peripheral devices
Tech Talk: The Windows Registry

This unit discusses computer hardware, with several lessons focusing on the various technologies that enable a computer to store and retrieve data and programs. Storage technology defines how computers store data and program files. You will learn the difference between magnetic storage and optical storage. You will learn about the components of a computer's expansion bus, including various types of expansion slots and cables and how to use the expansion bus to add devices to a computer. You will learn about input and output devices such as popular printer and display technologies, and you will get an in-depth look at the keyboard. You will learn about a variety of peripheral devices including how to install them, and how the Windows Registry tracks installed devices.

Introducing storage technology

The basic functions of a computer are to accept input, process data, store data, and produce output. When you want to store data permanently, you save the data to a storage device. Computers can be configured with a variety of storage devices, such as a floppy disk drive, hard disk drive, CD drive, or DVD drive. While one storage technology might provide extremely fast access to data, it might also be susceptible to problems that could wipe out all of your data. A different storage technology might be more dependable, but it might also have the disadvantage of providing relatively slow access to data. Understanding the strengths and weaknesses of each storage technology will enable you to use each device appropriately and with maximum effectiveness.

DETAILS

● The term **storage technology** refers to data storage systems. Each data storage system has two main components: a storage medium and a storage device. A **storage medium** (storage media is the plural) is the disk, tape, CD, DVD, paper, or other substance that holds data. See Figure B-1. A **storage device** is the mechanical apparatus that records and retrieves data from a storage medium. Storage devices include floppy disk drives, Zip drives, hard disk drives, tape drives, CD drives, and DVD drives. See Figure B-2.

● Data is copied from a storage device into RAM, where it waits to be processed. **RAM** (random access memory) is a temporary holding area for the operating system, the file you are working on (such as a word processing document), and application program instructions. RAM is not permanent storage, in fact RAM is very **volatile**, which means data in RAM can be lost easily. That is why it is important to store data permanently.

● RAM is important to the storage process. You can think of RAM as the connection between your computer's storage devices and their storage media. After data is processed in RAM, it is usually copied to a storage medium for more permanent safekeeping.

● The process of storing data is often referred to as "writing data" or "saving a file" because the storage device writes the data on the storage medium to save it for later use. The process of retrieving data is often referred to as "reading data," "loading data," or "opening a file."

● A computer works with data that has been coded and can be represented by 1s and 0s. When data is stored, these 1s and 0s must be converted into a signal or mark that's fairly permanent but that can be changed when necessary. The data is not literally written as "1" or "0." Instead, the 1s and 0s must be transformed to change the surface of a storage medium. Exactly how this transformation happens depends on the storage technology. For example, floppy disks store data in a different way than CD-ROMs.

The science of data representation

Letters, numbers, musical notes, and pictures don't pass from the keyboard through the circuitry of a computer and then jump out onto the screen or printer. So how is it that a computer can work with documents, photos, videos, and sound recordings? The answer to that question is what data representation and digital electronics are all about. Data representation is based on the binary number system, which uses two numbers, 1 and 0, to represent all data. Data representation makes it possible to convert letters, sounds, and images into electrical signals. Digital electronics makes it possible for a computer to manipulate simple "on" and "off" signals, which are represented by the 0s and 1s, to perform complex tasks.

FIGURE B-1: Examples of storage media

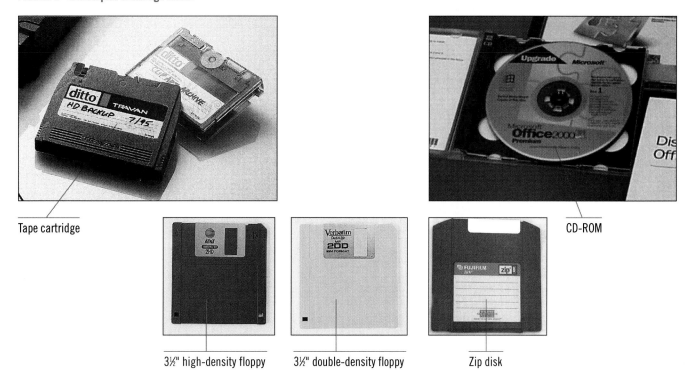

Tape cartridge

3½" high-density floppy

3½" double-density floppy

Zip disk

CD-ROM

FIGURE B-2: Examples of storage devices in a system unit

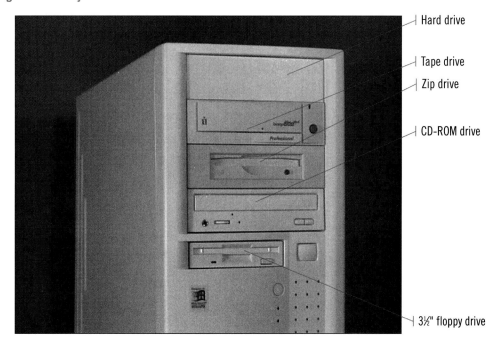

Hard drive

Tape drive

Zip drive

CD-ROM drive

3½" floppy drive

Comparing storage technologies

Currently there are two main categories of storage technologies: magnetic and optical. Each storage technology has advantages and disadvantages. To compare storage devices, you need to understand how each one works.

DETAILS

● Hard disk, floppy disk, Zip disk, and tape storage technologies can be classified as **magnetic storage**, which stores data by magnetizing microscopic particles on the disk or tape surface. The particles retain their magnetic orientation until that orientation is changed, thereby making disks and tape fairly permanent but modifiable storage media. A **read-write head** mechanism in the disk drive reads and writes the magnetized particles that represent data. Figure B-3 shows how a computer stores data on magnetic media.

● Before data is stored, the particles on the surface of the disk are scattered in random patterns. The disk drive's read-write head magnetizes the particles and orients them in either a positive or negative direction. These patterns of magnetized particles are interpreted as the 0s and 1s that represent data. Data stored magnetically can be changed or deleted simply by altering the magnetic orientation of the appropriate particles on the disk surface. This feature of magnetic storage provides flexibility for editing data and reusing areas of a storage medium containing data that is no longer needed.

● Magnetic media is not very durable. Data stored on magnetic media such as floppy disks can be altered by magnetic fields, dust, mold, smoke particles, heat, and mechanical problems with a storage device. For example, a magnet should never be placed on or near a floppy disk because it will destroy the magnetic particles on the disk. Magnetic media gradually lose their magnetic charge, which results in lost data. Some experts estimate that the reliable life span of data stored on magnetic media is about three years.

● CD and DVD storage technologies make use of **optical storage**, which stores data as microscopic light and dark spots on the disk surface. The dark spots are called **pits**, and it is possible to see the data stored on a CD or DVD storage medium using a high-powered microscope. See Figure B-4. The lighter, non-pitted surface areas of the disk are called **lands**. This type of storage is called optical storage because a low-power laser light is used to read the data stored on an optical disk. When the beam strikes a pit, no light is reflected. When the laser strikes a reflective surface, light bounces back into the read head. The patterns of light and dark between pits and lands are interpreted as the 1s and 0s that represent data. Data recorded on optical media is generally considered to be less susceptible to environmental damage than data recorded on magnetic media. The useful life of a CD-ROM disk is estimated to exceed 500 years.

FIGURE B-3: Magnetic storage

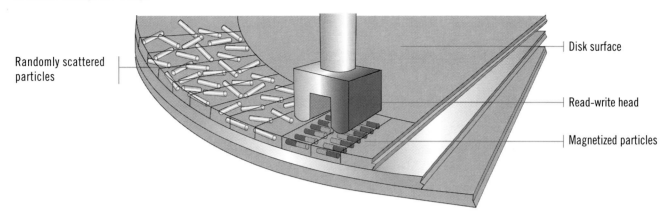

Randomly scattered particles

Disk surface

Read-write head

Magnetized particles

FIGURE B-4: Optical storage

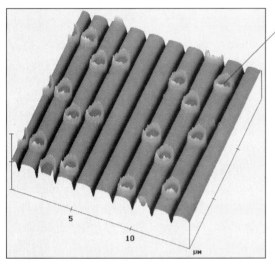

The pits on an optical storage disk as seen through an electron microscope; each pit is 1 micron in diameter

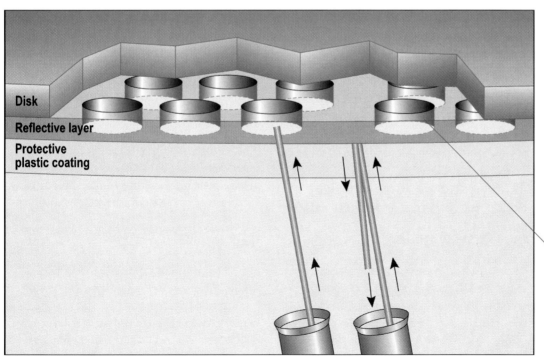

Disk

Reflective layer

Protective plastic coating

When a CD-ROM disk is manufactured, a laser burns pits into a reflective surface; these pits become dark non-reflective areas on the disk

Comparing storage media and devices

When trying to determine the best storage media for a job, it is useful to apply four criteria: versatility, durability, speed, and capacity. Versatility is the ability of a device and its media to work in more than one way. After storing data using this storage technology, can that data be changed? Durability determines the ability of the device or media to last. How long will it work? How long will the data be accessible? Speed is the time it takes to retrieve or access the data, a factor that is very important in determining how efficiently you work. Finally, capacity is the amount of data each technology can store.

DETAILS

FYI

Storage media is divided into tracks and then into sectors to create electronic "addressable bins" in which to store data.

- Versatility. Some storage devices can access data from only one type of medium. More versatile devices can access data from several different media. A floppy disk drive, for example, can access only floppy disks, but a DVD drive can access data DVDs, DVD movies, audio CDs, data CDs, and CD-Rs.

- Durability. Most storage technologies are susceptible to damage from mishandling or other environmental factors, such as heat and moisture. Some technologies are less susceptible than others. Optical technologies tend to be less susceptible than magnetic technologies to damage that could cause data loss.

- Speed. Not surprisingly, fast storage devices are preferred over slower ones. **Access time** is the average time it takes a computer to locate data on the storage medium and read it. Access time for a personal computer storage device, such as a disk drive, is measured in **milliseconds** (thousandths of a second). Lower numbers indicate faster access times. For example, a drive with a 6 ms access time is faster than a drive with an access time of 11 ms. Random-access devices have the fastest access times.

    Random access (also called "direct access") is the ability of a device to "jump" directly to the requested data. Floppy disk, hard disk, CD, and DVD

drives are random-access devices. A tape drive, on the other hand, must use slower **sequential access**, which reads through the data from the beginning of the tape. The advantage of random access becomes clear when you consider how much faster and easier it is to locate a song on a CD (random access) than on a cassette tape (sequential access).

    Data transfer rate is the amount of data that a storage device can move from the storage medium to the computer per second. Higher numbers indicate faster transfer rates. For example, a CD-ROM drive with a 600 KBps (kilobytes per second) data transfer rate is faster than one with a 300 KBps transfer rate.

- Capacity. **Storage capacity** is the maximum amount of data that can be stored on a storage medium, measured in kilobytes (KB), megabytes (MB), gigabytes (GB), or terabytes (TB). The amount of data that a disk stores—its capacity— depends on its density. **Disk density** refers to the closeness and size of the magnetic particles on the disk surface. The higher the disk density, the smaller the magnetic particles on the disk surface, and the more data it can store. Higher capacity is almost always preferred. Figure B-5 compares the capacity and costs of various storage devices and media.

Adding storage devices to a computer

Computer users frequently want to upgrade their hard drive to gain capacity or to add CD or DVD drives to make their system more versatile. The system unit case for a desktop computer contains several storage device "parking spaces" called **drive bays**. See Figure B-6. If you have an empty bay that is the right type and size, you can add a storage device. Bays come in two widths—5¼" and 3½". CD and DVD drives require 5¼" bays; a floppy disk drive fits in a 3½" bay. Some drive bays provide access from the outside of the system unit, a necessity for a storage device with removable media, such as floppy disks, CDs, tapes, and DVDs. Internal drive bays are located deep inside the system unit and are designed for hard disk drives, which don't use removable storage media.

FIGURE B-5: Storage capacities of backup media

	DEVICE COST	MEDIA COST	CAPACITY	COMMENTS
Floppy disk	$40-99	30¢	1.44 MB	Low capacity means that you have to wait around to feed in disks
Zip disk	$139 (average)	$11.00	250 MB	Holds much more than a floppy but a backup still requires multiple disks
Fixed hard disk	$150 (average)	-NA-	40 GB (average)	Fast and convenient, but risky because it is susceptible to damage or theft of your computer
Removable hard disk	$149 (average)	$30.00	2.2 GB (average)	Fast, limited capacity, but disks can be removed and locked in a secure location
CD-R	$130-200	50¢	680 MB	Limited capacity, can't be reused, long shelf life
CD-RW	$130-200	$1.50	680 MB	Limited capacity, reusable, very slow
Writable DVD	$500 (average)	$25.00	5.2 GB	Good capacity, not yet standardized
Tape	$199 (average)	$50.00	30 GB (average)	Great capacity, reasonable media cost, convenient—you can let backups run overnight

FIGURE B-6: Drive bays

An empty 5¼" drive bay located on the front of a desktop computer

An empty 3½" drive bay

An empty drive bay located on the side of a notebook computer

Exploring floppy disk technology

A **floppy disk** is a round piece of flexible mylar plastic covered with a thin layer of magnetic oxide and sealed inside a protective casing. If you broke open the disk casing (something you should never do unless you want to ruin the disk), you would see that the mylar disk inside is thin and literally floppy. See Figure B-7. Floppy disks are also referred to as "floppies" or "diskettes." It is not correct to call them "hard disks" even though they seem to have a "hard" or rigid plastic casing. The term "hard disk" refers to an entirely different storage technology.

Info Web
FLOPPY DISK
DRIVES

DETAILS

- Floppy disks come in many sizes and capacities. The floppies most commonly used on today's personal computers are 3½" disks with a capacity of 1.44 MB, which means they can store 1,440,000 bytes of data.

- A floppy disk features a **write-protect window**, which is a small square opening that can be covered by a moveable plastic tab on the disk. When you open the window, the disk is "write-protected," which means that a computer cannot write or save data on the disk.

- Two additional storage systems use floppy disk technology. **Zip disks**, manufactured by Iomega, are available in 100 MB and 250 MB versions. **SuperDisks**, a technology manufactured by Imation, have a capacity of 120 MB. Although the increased storage capacity of these types of disks is attractive, they require special disk drives; a standard floppy disk drive will not read them. SuperDisks, however, are backward-compatible with standard floppy disk technology, which means you can use a SuperDisk drive to read and write to standard floppy disks. Three types of floppy disk drives are shown in Figure B-8.

- The major advantage of floppy disks is their portability. Floppies are still used in many school computer labs so that students can transport their data to different lab machines or to their personal computers.

- A major disadvantage of standard 3½" floppy disks is their relatively low storage capacity. Files that students are creating, such as presentations with graphics and databases, are large. Often, these files will not fit on a 3½" floppy disk, making Zip disks, SuperDisks, or CDs that you can read from and write to (called CD-Rs) more attractive.

- Another disadvantage is that a standard 3½" floppy disk drive is not a particularly speedy device. It takes about 0.5 second for the drive to spin the disk up to maximum speed and find a specific sector that contains data. A Zip drive is about 20 times faster, but both are significantly slower than a hard disk drive.

- The limited storage capacity of floppy disks also makes them less attractive as a distribution medium. In the past, software was distributed on floppy disks. Today, most software vendors use CD-ROM or DVD-ROM disks instead. The Internet has also made it easy to share data files so floppy disks are shipped less frequently.

What HD DS and HDD mean

Today's floppies are "high-density disks" (HD or HDD). When you see "HD DS" on a box of floppy disks it means "high-density double-sided." Although the storage capacity of a standard floppy disk pales beside that of Zip and SuperDisks, there was a time when floppies stored even less. At one time, floppy disks stored data only on one side. Today, however, most store data on both sides. Read-write heads above and below the disk read both sides so that you don't have to turn the disk over.

FIGURE B-7: A 3½" floppy disk

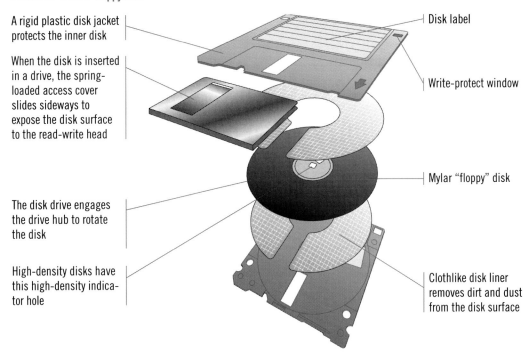

A rigid plastic disk jacket protects the inner disk

When the disk is inserted in a drive, the spring-loaded access cover slides sideways to expose the disk surface to the read-write head

The disk drive engages the drive hub to rotate the disk

High-density disks have this high-density indicator hole

Disk label

Write-protect window

Mylar "floppy" disk

Clothlike disk liner removes dirt and dust from the disk surface

FIGURE B-8: Inserting a floppy disk, a Zip disk, or a SuperDisk

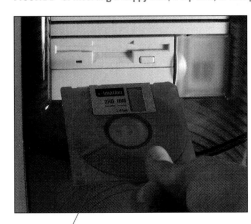

The storage device that records and retrieves data on a floppy disk is a floppy disk drive, shown here with a 3½" floppy disk

A Zip disk requires special disk drives, but is transportable and provides more storage capacity than a floppy disk

A SuperDisk provides an alternative high-capacity, transportable storage option; SuperDisk drives can read standard floppy disks, but a SuperDisk cannot be used in a standard floppy disk drive

Exploring hard disk technology

Hard disk technology is the preferred type of main storage for most computer systems. Hard disks provide more than enough storage capacity for most users and provide faster access to files than floppy disk drives do. In addition, hard disks are more economical than floppy disks. A hard disk typically stores millions of times more data than a floppy disk, but a hard disk drive might cost only three times as much as a floppy disk drive.

DETAILS

- A **hard disk** is one or more platters and their associated read-write heads. A **hard disk platter** is a flat, rigid disk made of aluminum or glass and coated with magnetic iron oxide particles. Personal computer hard disk platters are typically 3½" in diameter. This is the same size as the circular mylar disk in a floppy, but the density of the surface particles on hard disk platters far exceeds that of a floppy disk. You will frequently see the terms "hard disk" and "hard disk drive" used interchangeably. You might also hear the term "fixed disk" used to refer to hard disks.

- The data storage capacity of a hard disk far exceeds that of a floppy disk. Hard disk storage capacities of 40 GB and access times of 6 to 11 ms are not uncommon.

- The access time for a hard disk is significantly faster than that for a floppy disk. Hard disk drive speed is sometimes measured in **revolutions per minute** (rpm). The faster a drive spins, the more rapidly it can position the read-write head over specific data. For example, a 7,200 rpm drive is able to access data faster than a 5,400 rpm drive.

- Hard disk platters are divided into tracks and sectors into which data is written. You might guess that a hard disk drive would fill one platter before storing data on a second platter. However, it is more efficient to store data at the same track and sector locations on all platters before moving the read-write heads to the next sector. A vertical stack of tracks is called a **cylinder**, which is the basic storage bin for a hard disk drive. Figure B-9 provides more information on how a hard disk drive works.

- A hard drive storage device includes a circuit board, called a **controller,** which positions the disk and read-write heads to locate data. Disk drives are classified according to the type of controller they use. Popular drive controllers include Ultra ATA,

EIDE, and SCSI. **Ultra ATA (AT attachment)** and **EIDE (enhanced integrated drive electronics)** use essentially the same drive technology and feature high storage capacity and fast data transfer. Ultra ATA drives, which are commonly found in today's PCs, are twice as fast as their EIDE counterparts. **SCSI (small computer system interface)** drives provide a slight performance advantage over EIDE drives and are typically found in high-performance workstations and servers.

- Hard disks are not as durable as many other storage technologies. The read-write heads in a hard disk hover a microscopic distance above the disk surface. If a read-write head runs into a dust particle or some other contaminant on the disk, or if the hard disk is jarred while it is in use, it might cause a **head crash**. A head crash damages some of the data on the disk. To help prevent contaminants from contacting the platters and causing head crashes, a hard disk is sealed in its case.

- Removable hard disks or hard disk cartridges contain platters and read-write heads that can be inserted and removed from the drive much like floppy disks. Removable hard disks increase the storage capacity of your computer system, although the data is available on only one disk at a time. Removable hard disks also provide security for data by allowing you to remove the hard disk cartridge and store it separately from the computer.

- **RAID (redundant array of independent disks)** is another category of disk drive storage devices. RAID combines two or more drives containing many disk platters to provide redundancy and achieve faster data access than conventional hard disks. The redundancy feature of RAID technology protects data from media failures by recording the same data on more than one disk platter simultaneously. RAID is a popular option for mainframe and server storage but is less popular for personal computers.

FIGURE B-9: How a hard disk works

The drive spindle supports one or more hard disk platters; both sides of the platter are used for data storage; more platters mean more data storage capacity; hard disk platters rotate as a unit on the spindle to position read-write heads over specific data; the platters spin continuously, making thousands of rotations per minute

▲ Each data storage surface has its own read-write head, which moves in and out from the center of the disk to locate data; the head hovers only a few microinches above the disk surface, so the magnetic field is much more compact than on a floppy disk; as a result, more data is packed into a smaller area on a hard disk platter

Understanding tape storage

Tape is another type of storage technology; it consists of a tape for the storage medium and a tape drive for the storage device. Tape is a sequential, rather than a random-access, storage medium. Data is arranged as a long sequence of bits that begins at one end of the tape and stretches to the other end. As a result, tape access is much slower than hard drive access. In fact, access times for a tape are measured in seconds rather than in milliseconds. A tape may contain hundreds, or in the case of a mainframe, thousands of feet of tape.

The most popular types of tape drives for personal computers use tape cartridges for the storage medium. A **tape cartridge** is a removable magnetic tape module similar to a cassette tape. Figure B-10 shows several different kinds of tape used with personal computer tape drives.

Tape drives are available in either internal or external models. An internal tape drive fits into a standard drive bay. An external model is a stand-alone device that you can connect to your computer with a cable.

FIGURE B-10

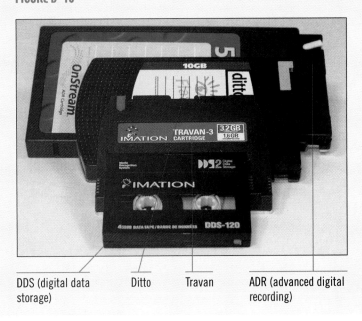

DDS (digital data storage)   Ditto   Travan   ADR (advanced digital recording)

Exploring CD/DVD technology

A CD-ROM drive is an optical storage device that is usually installed in one of the system unit's drive bays. **CD-ROM (compact disc read-only memory)** is based on the same technology as the audio CDs that contain your favorite music. Your computer can read data from a CD-ROM, but you can't store or record any of your own data on a CD-ROM disk. Two CD-writer technologies called CD-R and CD-RW allow you to create your own CDs. **DVD** ("digital video disc" or "digital versatile disk") is a variation of CD technology that was originally designed as an alternative to VCRs, but was quickly adopted by the computer industry to store data.

Info Web

CD and DVD

DETAILS

- A computer **CD-ROM disk**, like its audio counterpart, contains data that was stamped on the disk surface when it was manufactured. Today, when you purchase software from a computer store, the box typically contains CDs. Therefore, unless you plan to download all of your new software from the Internet, your computer should have a CD drive so that you can install new software. Figure B-11 shows how to place a CD in the drive. Figure B-12 illustrates how a CD-ROM drive uses laser technology to read data.

- CD-ROM technology provides a far larger storage capacity than floppy disks, Zip disks, or SuperDisks. A single CD-ROM disk holds up to 680 MB, equivalent to more than 300,000 pages of text. The surface of the disk is coated with a clear plastic, making the disk quite durable. Unlike magnetic media, the data on a CD-ROM is not susceptible to permanent damage by humidity, fingerprints, dust, or magnets.

- The original CD-ROM drives were able to access 150 KB of data per second. The next generation of drives doubled the data transfer rate and was consequently dubbed "2X"; and transfer rates are continually increasing. A 24X CD-ROM drive, for example, would transfer data at a rate of 24 × 150 KB, or 3,600 KB per second.

- A **CD-R (compact disc recordable)** drive records data on a special CD-R disk. The drive mechanism includes a laser that changes the reflectivity of a dye layer on a blank CD-R disk. As a result, the data on the disk is not actually stored in pits. Dark spots in the dye layer, however, play the same role as pits to represent data and allow the disks that you create to be read by not only a CD-R drive, but also by a standard CD-ROM or DVD

drive. The data on a CD-R cannot be erased or modified once recorded, but most CD-R drives allow you to record your data in multiple sessions.

- **CD-RW (compact disc rewritable)** technology allows you to write data on a CD and change that data at a later time. The process requires special CD-RW disks and a CD-RW drive, which uses phase change technology to alter the crystal structure on the disk surface. Altering the crystal structure creates patterns of light and dark spots similar to the pits and lands on a CD-ROM disk. The crystal structure can be changed from light to dark and back again many times, making it possible to record and modify data much like you can with a hard disk or a floppy disk. However, accessing, saving, and modifying data on a CD-RW disk is slower than on a hard disk.

- Both CD-R and CD-RW technologies are quite useful for archiving data and distributing large files. **Archiving** refers to the process of removing infrequently used data from a primary storage device to another storage medium, such as a CD-R.

- A computer's DVD drive can read disks that contain computer data (often called **DVD-ROM** disks) and disks that contain DVD movies (sometimes called DVD-Video disks). A DVD holds about 4.7 GB (4,700 MB), compared with 680 MB on a CD-ROM. Like a CD-ROM disk, a DVD-ROM disk is permanently stamped with data at the time of manufacture, so you cannot add or change data. The speed of a DVD drive is measured on a different scale than a CD drive. A 1X DVD drive is about the same speed as a 9X CD drive. Table B-1 provides additional speed equivalents.

Using DVD technologies

A computer DVD drive is not exactly the same as one that's connected to a television set. Even with the large storage capacity of a DVD, movie files are much too large to fit on a disk unless they are compressed, using a special type of data coding called **MPEG-2**. The DVD player that you connect to your television includes MPEG decoding circuitry, which is not included on your computer's

DVD drive. When you play DVD movies on your computer, it uses the CPU as an MPEG decoder. The necessary decoder software is included with Windows, or can be located on the DVD itself. You cannot play DVDs on your CD-ROM drive, but you can play CD-ROM, most CD-R, and most CD-RW disks on your DVD drive.

FIGURE B-11: Inserting a CD-ROM

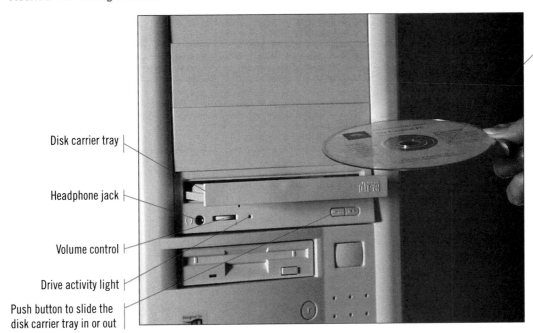

Disk carrier tray

Headphone jack

Volume control

Drive activity light

Push button to slide the disk carrier tray in or out

Data is stored on the bottom of a CD-ROM disk in one continuous track that spirals out from the center of the disk; the track is divided into equal-length sectors; the printed side of the disk does not contain data; it should be face up when you insert the disk because the lasers read the bottom of the disk

FIGURE B-12: How a CD-ROM drive works

Laser lens directs a beam of light to the underside of the CD-ROM disk

Tracking mechanism positions a disk track over the laser lens

Drive spindle spins disk

Laser pickup assembly senses the reflectivity of pits and lands

TABLE B-1: Comparing DVD and CD speeds

DVD DRIVE SPEED	DATA TRANSFER RATE	CD SPEED
1X	11.08 Mbps	9X
2X	22.16 Mbps	18X
4X	44.32 Mbps	36X
5X	55.40 Mbps	46X

Understanding expansion slots, cards, ports, and cables

Within a computer, data travels from one component to another over circuits called a **data bus**. One part of the data bus runs between RAM and the microprocessor; the other part runs between RAM and various storage devices. The segment of the data bus between RAM and peripheral devices is called the **expansion bus**. As data moves along the expansion bus, it may travel through expansion slots, cards, ports, and cables.

DETAILS

- An **expansion slot** is a long, narrow socket on the motherboard into which you can plug an expansion card. The motherboard is the main board in the computer that holds the components that control the processing functions. An **expansion card** is a small circuit board that provides a computer the ability to control a storage device, an input device, or an output device. Expansion cards are also called "expansion boards," "controller cards," or "adapters." To insert an expansion card, you slide it into an expansion slot, where it can be secured with a small screw. See Figure B-13.

- Most desktop computers have four to eight expansion slots, but some of the slots usually contain expansion cards. A **graphics card** (sometimes called a "video card") provides a path for data traveling to the monitor. A **modem card** provides a way to transmit data over phone lines or cable television lines. A **sound card** carries data out to speakers and headphones, or back from a microphone. A **network card** allows you to connect your computer to a local area network. You might add other expansion cards if you want to connect a scanner or download videos from a camera or VCR.

- A desktop computer may have up to three types of expansion slots. Each expansion card is built for only one type of slot. AGP, PCI, and ISA slots are different lengths so you can easily identify them by opening your computer's system unit and looking at the motherboard. See Figure B-14. **ISA (industry standard architecture)** slots are an old technology, used today only for some modems and other relatively slow devices. **PCI (peripheral component interconnect)** slots offer fast transfer speeds and a 32-bit or 64-bit data bus. This type of slot typically houses a graphics card, sound card, video capture card, modem, or network interface card. **AGP (accelerated graphics port)** slots provide a high-speed data pathway that is primarily used for graphics cards.

- Most notebook computers are equipped with a special type of external slot called a **PCMCIA slot (personal computer memory card international association)**. Typically, a notebook computer has only one of these slots, but the slot can hold more than one PC card (also called "PCMCIA expansion cards" or "Card Bus cards"). PCMCIA slots are classified according to their thickness. Type 1 slots accept only the thinnest PC cards, such as memory expansion cards. Type II slots accept most of the popular PC cards such as those that contain modems, sound cards, and network cards. Type III slots commonly included with today's notebook computers accept the thickest PC cards, which contain devices such as hard disk drives. A Type III slot can also hold two Type 1 cards, two Type II cards, or a Type 1 and a Type II card. Figure B-15 shows a PCMCIA slot and a PC card.

- An **expansion port** is any connector that passes data in and out of a computer or peripheral device. See Figure B-16. Ports are sometimes called "jacks" or "connectors," but the terminology is inconsistent. An expansion port is often housed on an expansion card so that it is accessible through an opening in the back of the computer's system unit. A port might also be built into the system unit case of a desktop or notebook computer. The built-in ports on a computer usually include a mouse port, keyboard port, serial port, and USB port. Ports that have been added with expansion cards usually protrude through rectangular cutouts in the back of the case.

- If a **cable** is supplied with a peripheral device, you can usually figure out where to plug it in by matching the shape of the cable connector to the port. If you need to purchase a cable, be sure the cable matches the available ports.

FIGURE B-13: Inserting an expansion card

FIGURE B-14: Types of expansion slots

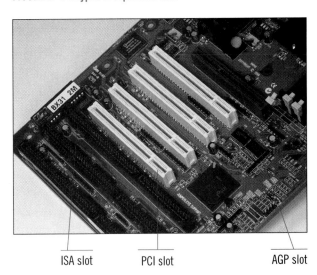

ISA slot   PCI slot   AGP slot

FIGURE B-15: PC card for a notebook computer

PC card

FIGURE B-16: Expansion ports on a typical desktop computer

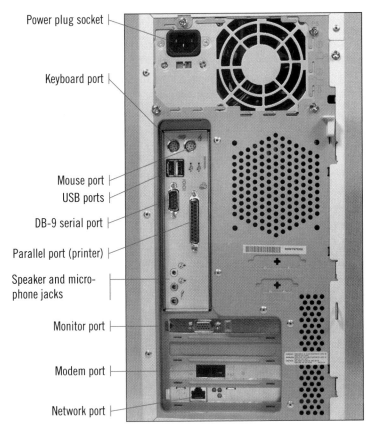

Power plug socket

Keyboard port

Mouse port

USB ports

DB-9 serial port

Parallel port (printer)

Speaker and micro-
phone jacks

Monitor port

Modem port

Network port

Comparing display devices

A computer display system is the main output device for a computer. Two key components of a computer display system are a graphics card and a display device, such as a monitor or LCD screen.

Info Web
DISPLAY DEVICES

DETAILS

- A **graphics card** (also called a "graphics board" or a "video card") contains circuitry that generates the signals for displaying an image on the screen. It also contains special video memory, which stores screen images as they are processed before they are displayed. Today's fastest graphics cards fit in an AGP expansion slot. PCI graphics cards typically take a bit longer to update the screen. Many graphics cards contain special graphics accelerator technology to boost performance for 3-D graphics applications, including computer games.

- For many years, CRT monitors were the only game in town for desktop computer displays. **CRT (cathode ray tube)** technology uses gun-like mechanisms to direct beams of electrons toward the screen and activate individual dots of color that form an image – much like a color TV. CRT monitors offer an inexpensive and dependable computer display.

- As an alternative to CRT monitors, an **LCD (liquid crystal display)** monitor produces an image by manipulating light within a layer of liquid crystal cells. Modern LCD technology is compact in size, lightweight, and easy to read. While LCDs are standard equipment on notebook computers, newer notebooks feature an **active matrix screen**, sometimes referred to as "TFT" (thin film transistor), which updates rapidly and is essential for crisp display of animations and video. Consumers might pay more for a notebook with TFT technology. Recently, stand-alone LCDs, referred to as "LCD monitors" or "flat panel displays," have also become available for desktop computers.

- The advantages of an LCD monitor include display clarity (even in sunlit rooms), low radiation emission, portability, and compactness. However, there are several disadvantages. An LCD monitor can be triple the price of an equivalent CRT monitor. LCD monitors have a limited viewing angle; the brightness and color tones that you see depend on the angle from which you view the screen because of the way that light reflects off the LCD screen. Graphic artists prefer CRT technology, which displays uniform color from any viewing angle.

- Image quality is determined by screen size, dot pitch, resolution, and color depth. **Screen size** is the measurement in inches from one corner of the screen diagonally across to the opposite corner. Typical monitor screen sizes range from 13" to 21". On most monitors, the viewable image does not stretch to the edge of the screen. Instead, a black border makes the viewing area smaller than the screen size. Many computer ads now include a measurement of the **viewable image size (vis)**. A 15" monitor has an approximately 13.9" vis, as shown in Figure B-17.

- **Dot pitch** (dp) is a measure of image clarity. A smaller dot pitch means a crisper image. Technically, dot pitch is the distance in millimeters between like-colored pixels, the small dots of light that form an image. A dot pitch between .26 and .23 is typical for today's monitors.

- The computer's graphics card sends an image to the monitor at a specific **resolution**, defined as the maximum number of horizontal and vertical pixels that are displayed on the screen. Standard resolutions include 640 × 480, 800 × 600, and 1024 × 768. Even higher resolutions, such as 1600 × 1200, are possible given enough memory on the graphics card and a monitor capable of displaying that resolution. At higher resolutions, the computer displays a larger work area, such as an entire page of a document, but text and other objects appear smaller. The two screen shots in Figure B-18 help you compare a display at 640 × 480 resolution with a display at 1024 × 768 resolution.

- The number of colors that a monitor and graphics card can display is referred to as **color depth** or "**bit depth**." Most PCs have the capability to display millions of colors. When you set the resolution at 24-bit color depth (sometimes called "True Color"), your PC can display more than 16 million colors and produce what are considered photographic-quality images. Windows allows you to select resolution and color depth simply by right-clicking an empty area of the desktop, selecting Properties on the shortcut menu, selecting the Settings tab, and then changing the settings to meet your needs. Most desktop owners choose 24-bit color at 1024 × 768 resolution.

- Although you can set the color depth and resolution of your notebook computer display, you might not have as many options as you do with a desktop computer. Typically, the graphics card circuitry is built into the motherboard of a notebook computer, making it difficult to upgrade and gain more video memory for additional resolution and color depth.

FIGURE B-18: Comparing screen resolutions

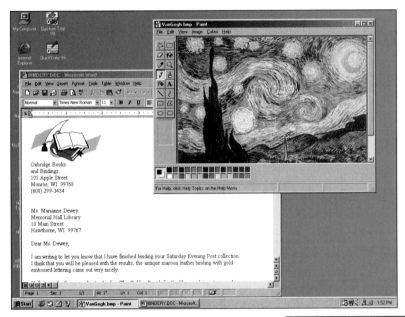

◀ Computer display set at
1024 × 768 resolution

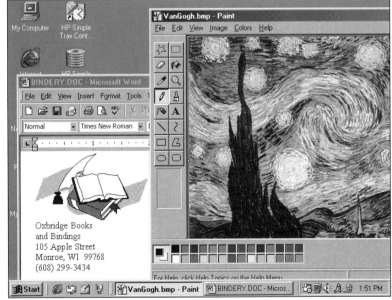

▶ Computer display set at 640 × 480 resolution; text and
other objects appear larger than on the high-resolution screen,
but you see a smaller portion of the screen-based desktop

Comparing printers

Printer technologies include ink jet, solid ink, thermal transfer, dye sublimation, laser, and dot matrix. Printers differ in resolution and speed, both of which affect the print quality and price. Most ink jet printers are small, lightweight, and inexpensive, yet produce very good quality color output. Laser printers are a popular technology for situations that require high-volume output or good-quality printouts. A dot matrix printer uses a grid of thin wires to strike a ribbon and create an image on paper. Unlike laser and ink-jet technologies, a dot matrix printer actually strikes the paper and, therefore, can print multipart carbon forms.

Info Web

PRINTER BUYER'S GUIDE

DETAILS

The quality or sharpness of printed images and text depends on the printer's resolution, the density of the grid of dots that create an image. Printer resolution is measured by the number of dots it can print per linear inch, abbreviated as **dpi**. At normal reading distance, a resolution of about 900 dots per inch appears solid to the human eye, but a close examination of color sections will reveal a dot pattern. Expensive coffee-table books are typically produced on printers with 2,400 dpi or higher.

Printer speeds are measured either by pages per minute (ppm) or characters per second (cps). Color printouts typically take longer than black-and-white printouts. Pages that contain mostly text tend to print more rapidly than pages that contain graphics. Ten pages per minute is a typical speed for a personal computer printer.

Ink jet printers (see Figure B-19) outsell all of the others because they produce low-cost color or black-and-white printouts. An **ink jet printer** has a nozzle-like print head that sprays ink onto paper to form characters and graphics. You must periodically replace the black ink cartridge and a second cartridge that carries the colored inks. Ink jet printers have excellent resolution, which can range from 600 dpi to 2,880 dpi, depending on the model. Some ink jet printers can produce ultra-high resolution by making multiple passes over the paper.

A **solid ink printer** melts sticks of crayon-like ink and then sprays the liquefied ink through the print head's tiny nozzles. The ink solidifies before the paper can absorb it, and a pair of rollers finishes fusing the ink onto the paper. A solid ink printer produces vibrant colors on most types of paper, so unlike an ink jet printer, it does not require special, expensive paper to produce photographic-quality images.

A **thermal transfer printer** uses a page-sized ribbon that is coated with cyan, magenta, yellow, and black wax. The print head consists of thousands of tiny heating elements that melt the wax onto specially coated paper or transparency film (the kind used for overhead projectors). This type of printer excels at printing colorful transparencies for presentations, but the fairly

expensive per-page costs and the requirement for special paper make this a niche market printer used mainly by businesses.

A **dye sublimation printer** uses technology similar to wax transfer. The difference is that the page-sized ribbon contains dye instead of colored wax. Heating elements in the print head diffuse the dye onto the surface of specially coated paper. Dye sublimation printers produce excellent color quality – perhaps the best of any printer technology. A high cost per page, however, makes these printers a bit pricey.

A **laser printer** (see Figure B-20) uses the same technology as a photocopier to produce dots of light on a light-sensitive drum. Personal laser printers produce six to eight ppm (pages per minute) at a resolution of 600 dpi. Professional models pump out 15 to 25 ppm at 1,200 dpi. A personal laser printer has a duty cycle of about 3,000 pages per month, which means roughly 100 pages per day.

Laser printers accept print commands from a personal computer, but use their own printer language to construct a page before printing it. **Printer Control Language (PCL)** is the most widely used printer language, but some printers use the PostScript language, which is preferred by many publishing professionals. Printer languages require memory, and most laser printers have between 2 MB and 8 MB. A large memory capacity is required to print color images and graphics-intensive documents. A laser printer comes equipped with enough memory for typical print jobs. If you find that you need more memory, check the printer documentation for information.

When PCs first began to appear in the late 1970s, dot matrix printers were the technology of choice, and they are still available today. A **dot matrix printer** (see Figure B-21) produces characters and graphics by using a grid of fine wires. Dot matrix speed is typically measured in characters per second (cps). A fast dot matrix device can print at speeds up to 455 cps or about five pages per minute. Today dot matrix printers are used primarily for "back-office" applications that demand low operating cost and dependability but not high print quality.

FIGURE B-19: Ink jet printer

▶ The print head in a color ink jet printer consists of a series of nozzles, each with its own ink cartridge; most ink jet printers use **CMYK color**, which requires only cyan (blue), magenta (pink), yellow, and black inks to create a printout that appears to have thousands of colors; alternatively, some printers use six ink colors to print midtone shades that create slightly more realistic photographic images

FIGURE B-20: Laser printer

Electrostatically charged ink is applied to the drum, then transferred to paper

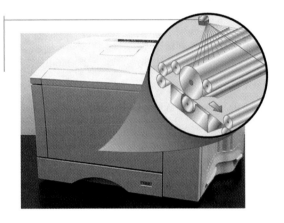

FIGURE B- 21: A dot matrix printer

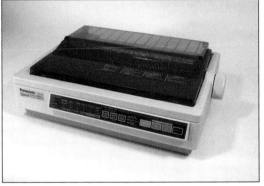

◀ Dot matrix printers can print text and graphics; some even print in color using a multicolored ribbon; with a resolution of 140 dpi, a dot matrix printer produces low-quality output with clearly discernible dots forming lettters and graphics

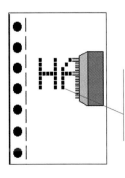

As the print head moves across the paper, the wires strike the ribbon and paper in a pattern prescribed by your PC

Examining keyboards

Most computers are equipped with a keyboard as the primary input device. A computer keyboard includes keys or buttons with letters and numbers as well as several keys with special characters and special words to control computer-specific tasks. Virtually every computer user interface requires you to use a keyboard. Although you don't have to be a great typist to use a computer effectively, you should be familiar with the computer keyboard and its special keys. Figure B-22 shows the location of the keys on a standard computer keyboard.

DETAILS

- You use the keys to input commands, respond to prompts, and type the text of documents. A cursor or an insertion point indicates where the characters you type will appear. The **cursor** appears on the screen as a flashing underline. The **insertion point** appears on the screen as a flashing vertical bar. You can change the location of the cursor or insertion point using the arrow keys or the mouse.

- The **numeric keypad** provides you with a calculator-style input device for numbers and arithmetic symbols. You can type numbers using either the set of number keys at the top of the keyboard or the keys on the numeric keypad. Notice that some keys on the numeric keypad contain two symbols. When the Num Lock key is activated, the numeric keypad will produce numbers. When the Num Lock key is not activated, the keys on the numeric keypad move the cursor in the direction indicated by the arrows on the keys.

  The Num Lock key is an example of a toggle key. A **toggle key** switches back and forth between two modes. The Caps Lock key is also a toggle key. When you press the Caps Lock key, you switch or "toggle" into uppercase mode. When you press the Caps Lock key again you toggle back into lowercase mode.

- **Function keys**, those keys numbered F1 through F12, are located either at the top or along the side of your keyboard. They were added to computer keyboards to help you initiate commands.

For example, with many software packages, you press the [F1] key to get help. The problem with function keys is that they are not standardized. In one program, you might press [F7] to save a document; but in another program, you might press [F5] to perform the same task.

- **Modifier keys**, the [Ctrl] (Control), [Alt], and [Shift] keys are located at the periphery of the typing keypad. There are 12 function keys, but you usually need more than 12 commands to control software. Therefore, you can use the [Ctrl], [Alt], and [Shift] keys in conjunction with the function keys to expand the repertoire of available commands. The [Alt] and [Ctrl] modifier keys also work in conjunction with the letter keys. Instead of using the mouse, you might use the [Alt] or [Ctrl] keys in combination with letter keys to access menu options. Such combinations are called **keyboard shortcuts**. If you see Alt+F1, [Alt F1], Alt-F1, or Alt F1 on the screen or in an instruction manual, it means to hold down the [Alt] key and press [F1] at the same time. You might see similar notations for using the [Ctrl] or [Shift] keys. In many Windows programs, [Ctrl]+X works as a keyboard shortcut to cut a selection and place it on the Clipboard, [Ctrl]+V works as a keyboard shortcut to paste the contents of the Clipboard at the insertion point, and [Ctrl]+C works as a keyboard shortcut to copy selected contents so that you can paste that information at the insertion point.

FIGURE B-22: The computer keyboard

The Esc or "escape" key cancels an operation

Each time you press the Backspace key, one character to the left of the insertion point is deleted

The Print Screen key either prints the contents of the screen or stores a copy of your screen in memory that you can manipulate or print with graphics software

The function of the Scroll Lock key depends on the software you are using; this key is rarely used with today's software

Indicator lights show you the status of each toggle key: Num Lock, Caps Lock, and Scroll Lock; the Power light indicates whether the computer is on or off

Function keys execute commands, such as saving a document; the command associated with each function key depends on the software you are using

The Insert key toggles between insert mode and typeover mode

The Num Lock key is a toggle key that switches between number keys and arrow keys on the numeric keypad

The Caps Lock key capitalizes all the letters you type when it is engaged, but does not produce the top symbol on keys that contain two symbols

You hold down the Ctrl or the Alt key while you press another key; the result of Ctrl key or Alt key combinations depends on the software you are using

The Home key takes you to the beginning of a line or the beginning of a document, depending on the software you are using

The arrow keys move the insertion point

The Page Up key displays the previous screen of information; the Page Down key displays the next screen of information

You hold down the Shift key while you press another key; the Shift key capitalizes letters and produces the top symbol on keys that contain two symbols

The End key takes you to the end of the line or the end of a document, depending on the software you are using

Alternative keyboard designs

In addition to the standard keyboard, innovative alternatives are becoming available. For example, some keyboards come with Internet hot keys. These keyboards have special keys that let you instantly access favorite Internet activities such as e-mailing, shopping, or searching the Web. Another alternative is an ergonomically designed keyboard, such as the one shown in Figure B-23, which may prevent computer, stress-related wrist injuries.

FIGURE B-23

Exploring peripheral devices

All computers use peripheral devices to input, output, and store data. **Peripheral devices** are equipment that you connect to the computer to enhance its functionality. They are hardware components that are "outside," or in addition to, the main computer.

DETAILS

● Although the keyboard, printer, monitor, disk drives, and mouse can be considered peripheral devices, they come standard and are necessary to operate basic computer functions. Other peripheral devices expand and modify your system. Figure B-24 shows examples of several peripheral devices. A **computer projection device** is an output device that produces a large display of the information shown on the computer screen. A **scanner** is an input device that converts a page of text or images into a digital format. A **digital camera** is an input device that records an image in digital format. **Multifunction devices** work both as input and output devices to combine the functions of a printer, scanner, copier, fax, and answering machine. A **graphics tablet** is an input device that accepts input from a pressure-sensitive stylus and converts strokes into images on the screen. A **trackball** and **joystick** are pointing devices that you use as alternative input devices to a mouse. **Track points** and **touchpads** are alternative input devices often found on notebook computers.

● The basic qualifications for installing peripheral devices are the ability to use a screwdriver and read directions. If you own a desktop computer, you might have to open the system unit. You should unplug the computer and ground yourself by using a special grounding wristband to release static electricity, or by touching both hands to a metal object. Simply follow the directions to install any necessary expansion cards and plug in the required cables. Most connectors have a shape-and-pin designation such as DB-9 or C-50. The first part of the designation indicates the shape of the connector. For example, DB and C connectors are trapezoidal, whereas DIN connectors are round. The second part of the designation indicates the number of pins. A DB-9 connector has nine pins. Figure B-25 describes the cable connectors you might need to connect a peripheral device to your PC.

● Some devices require software called a **device driver** to set up communication between your computer and the device. The directions supplied with your new peripheral device will include instructions on how to install the device driver. Typically, you'll use the device driver disk or CD once to get everything set up, then you can put the disk away. Be sure to keep the driver disk or CD in a safe place, however, because if you ever need to restore your computer or reinstall the device, you may need to install the driver again.

● Today's PCs include a feature called **Plug and Play** (also known as **PnP**) that automatically takes care of technical details for installing just about every popular peripheral device. If PnP doesn't work, your computer simply won't recognize the device and won't be able to transmit data to it or receive data from it. You can check the manufacturer's Web site for a device driver update or call the manufacturer's technical support department.

● After the device is connected using a cable and it is recognized by your computer, you then install the software based on Plug and Play technology. For example: most printers include a cable that connects to one of your computer's ports. A **parallel port** is most commonly used, but some printers are designed to connect to a USB port or a serial port. Many printers come packaged with device driver software, which provides access to the drivers needed to get your printer up and running. If your computer uses Windows, you'll probably have to use the Start button to access the Printers window, where you can select the newly installed printer as the "default printer" – the one you will use regularly.

FIGURE B-24: Examples of peripheral devices

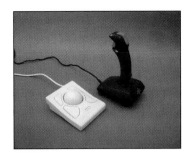

▲ Trackball and joystick

▲ Graphics tablet

▲ Scanner

▲ Multifunction device

▲ Computer projection device

▲ Digital camera

FIGURE B-25: Personal computer cables and connectors

	CONNECTOR	DESCRIPTION	DEVICES
	Serial DB-9	Connects to serial port, which sends data over a single data line one bit at a time at speeds of 56 Kbps.	Mouse or modem
	Parallel DB-25M	Connects to parallel port, which sends data simultaneously over 8 data lines at speeds of 12,000 Kbps.	Printer, external CD-ROM drive, Zip drive, external hard disk drive, or tape backup device
	USB	Connects to universal serial bus (USB), which sends data over a single data line at speeds of 12,000 Kbps and can support up to 127 devices.	Modem, keyboards, joystick, scanner, mouse
	SCSI C-50F	Connects to SCSI ("scuzzy") port, which sends data simultaneously over 8 or 16 data lines at speeds between 40,000 Kbps and 640,000 Kbps; supports up to 16 devices.	Hard disk drive, scanner, CD-ROM drive, tape backup device
	IEEE 1394	Connects to the "FireWire" port, which sends data at 400,000 Kbps.	Video camera, DVD player
	VGA HDB-15	Connects to the video port.	Monitor

The Windows Registry

To many computer owners, the Windows Registry is simply a mysterious "black box" that is mentioned occasionally in articles about computer troubleshooting. It is certainly possible to use a computer without intimate knowledge of the Registry, but it is useful to understand that the Registry is the "glue" that binds together many of the most important components of a PC: the computer hardware, peripheral devices, application software, and system software. After reading this Tech Talk section, you should have a basic understanding of the Registry and its role in the operation of a computer system.

Why does a PC need the Registry? You know that you use application software to direct the operations that a computer carries out. For some operations, particularly those that involve hardware, the application software communicates with the operating system. The operating system might communicate with device drivers or, in some cases, it can communicate directly with a peripheral device.

In order to act as an intermediary between software and peripheral devices, your operating system needs information about these components: where they are located, what's been installed, how they are configured, and how you want to use them. A special type of memory called **CMOS memory** holds the most essential data about your computer's processing and storage hardware, but the **Windows Registry** keeps track of your computer's peripheral devices and software so that the operating system can access the information it needs to coordinate the activities of the entire computer system. Some examples of specific data that the Registry tracks include your preferences for desktop colors, icons, pointers, shortcuts, and display resolution; the sounds that are assigned to various system events, such as clicking and shutting down; the capability of your CD-ROM drive for playing audio CDs and autorunning computer CDs; the options that appear on a shortcut menu when you right-click an object; your computer's network card settings and protocols; and the location of the uninstall routines for all installed hardware and software.

The contents of the Registry are stored in multiple files in the Windows/System folder of your computer's hard disk and are combined into a single database when Windows starts. Although each version of Windows uses a slightly different storage scheme, the basic organization and function of the Registry is similar in all versions.

Windows stores the entire contents of the Registry in two files: System.dat and User.dat. System.dat includes configuration data for all the hardware and software installed on a computer. User.dat contains user-specific information, sometimes called a "user profile," which includes software settings and desktop settings.

The Registry has a logical structure that appears as a hierarchy of folders, as shown in Figure B-26. There are six main folders in the Registry, and their names begin with HKEY. Each folder contains data that pertains to a particular part of a computer system.

You indirectly change the Registry whenever you install or remove hardware or software. Device drivers and the Windows Plug and Play feature automatically update the Registry with essential information about the hardware's location and configuration. The setup program for your software provides similar update services for newly installed software.

You can also make changes to the Windows Registry by using the dialog boxes for various configuration routines provided by the operating system and application software. For example, if you want to change the desktop colors for your user profile, you can do so by selecting the Settings option from the Start menu, clicking Control Panel, and then selecting the Display option. Any changes that you make to the settings in the Display Properties dialog box (Figure B-27) will be recorded in the Windows Registry.

FIGURE B-26: The Windows Registry

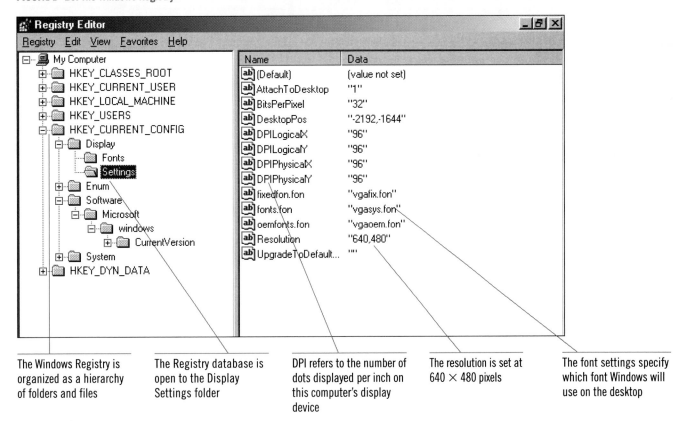

The Windows Registry is organized as a hierarchy of folders and files

The Registry database is open to the Display Settings folder

DPI refers to the number of dots displayed per inch on this computer's display device

The resolution is set at 640 × 480 pixels

The font settings specify which font Windows will use on the desktop

FIGURE B-27: Display properties

▶ Changes that you make when using the Display Properties dialog box will automatically update the corresponding entries in the HKEY_CURRENT_CONFIG folder of the Registry

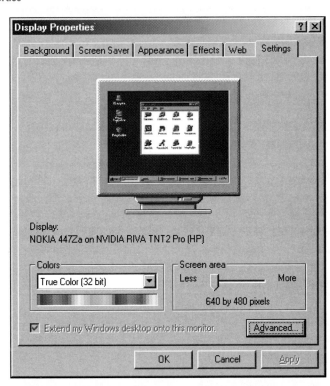

Why Recycle Computers?

Keeping up with technology means replacing your computer every few years, but what should you do with your old, outdated computer? According to the National Safety Council, an estimated 350 million computers will be obsolete by the year 2005, and more than 55 million of those computers are expected to end up in landfills. It is estimated that U.S. landfills already hold more than 2 million tons of computer parts, which contain toxic substances such as lead, phosphorus, and mercury. A computer monitor can contain up to six pounds of lead.

An Environmental Protection Agency (EPA) report sums up the situation: "In this world of rapidly changing technology, disposal of computers and other electronic equipment has created a new and growing waste stream."

Many computers end up in landfills because their owners were unaware of potential environmental hazards and simply tossed them in the garbage. In addition, PC owners typically are not provided with information concerning the options for disposing of their old machines. Instead of throwing away your old computer, you might be able to sell it; donate it to a local school, church, or community program; have it hauled away by a professional recycling firm; or send it back to the manufacturer.

With the growing popularity of Internet auctions and dedicated computer reclamation sites, you might be able to get some cash for your old computer. At Web sites, such as the Computer Recycle Center (www.recycles.com), you can post an ad for your "old stuff." Off the Web, you can find several businesses, such as Computer Renaissance, that refurbish old computers and sell them in retail stores.

Donating your old computer to a local organization doesn't actually eliminate the disposal problem, but it does delay it. Unfortunately, finding a new home for an old computer is not always easy. Most schools and community organizations have few resources for repairing broken equipment, so if your old computer is not in good working order, it could be more of a burden than a gift. In addition, your computer might be too old to be compatible with the other computers that are used in an organization. It helps if you can donate software along with your old computer. To provide a legal transfer, include the software distribution disks, manuals, and license agreement. And remember, once you donate the software, you cannot legally use it on your new computer unless it is freeware or shareware. If you cannot find an organization to accept your computer donation, look in your local Yellow Pages or on the Internet for an electronics recycling firm that will haul away your computer and recycle any usable materials.

Despite the private sector options for selling, donating, or recycling old computers, many governments are worried that these "voluntary" efforts will not be enough to prevent massive dumping of an ever-growing number of obsolete computers. Many lawmakers in the United States, Japan, and the European Union believe that legislation is necessary, but they can't agree on an implementation plan. Basic to the issue is the question of "Who pays?" Should it be the taxpayer, the individual consumer, or the computer manufacturer?

Currently, taxpayers pick up the tab for electronic waste disposal through municipal trash pick-up fees or local taxes. But is this approach fair to individual taxpayers who generate very little electronic waste? To make consumers responsible for the cost of recycling the products that they buy, some lawmakers suggest adding a special recycling tax to computers and other electronic devices. A proposal in South Carolina, for example, would impose a $5 fee on the sale of each piece of electronic equipment containing a CRT, and require the state treasurer to deposit the fees into a recycling fund for electronic equipment.

Other lawmakers propose making manufacturers responsible for recycling costs and logistics. "Extended producer responsibility" refers to the idea of holding manufacturers responsible for the environmental effects of their products through the entire product life cycle, which includes taking them back, recycling them, or disposing of them. Proposed legislation in Europe would require manufacturers to accept returns of their old equipment free of charge, then take appropriate steps to recycle it. The economics of a mandatory take-back program are likely to increase the costs of products because manufacturers would typically pass on recycling costs to consumers.

Some companies currently participate in voluntary extended producer responsibility programs. Hewlett-Packard, 3M, Nortel, Frigidaire, IBM, Sony, and Xerox, for example, provide recycling options for some products and components. Sony recently implemented a take-back program in Minnesota that allows residents to recycle all Sony products at no cost for the next five years. IBM recently implemented its PC Recycling Service program, which allows you to ship any make of computer, including system units, monitors, printers, and optional attachments, to a recycling center for a nominal fee. These programs and others are important steps in the effort to keep our planet green.

▼ EXPAND THE IDEAS

1. Have you ever thrown away an old computer or other electronic device? If so, how did you dispose of it? Did you donate it, pass it along, or just throw it in the garbage? Write a short essay explaining what your options were at the time, any thoughts about recycling or donating you might have had, and exactly how you got rid of the old computer.

2. Research options for recycling electronic equipment in your local area. Create a chart showing ways to get rid of an old computer, include the positive and negative aspects of each option. Include specific details for recycling or donating the computers, such as names or addresses.

3. Would it be fair for consumers to pay a recycling tax on any electronic equipment that they purchase? Research the current trends. Include any important legislation or pending legislation in your area or around the world that you feel is relevant. Compile your findings in a short report. Include your opinion in the conclusion.

Issue

End of Unit Exercises

▼ KEY TERMS

Access time
Active matrix screen
AGP
Archiving
Bit depth
Cable
CD-R
CD ROM
CD ROM disk
CD-RW
CMOS memory
Color depth
Computer projection device
Controller
CRT
Cursor
Cylinder
Data bus
Data transfer rate
Device driver
Digital camera
Disk density
Dot matrix printer
Dot pitch

Dpi
Drive bay
DVD
DVD-ROM
Dye sublimation printer
EIDE
Expansion bus
Expansion card
Expansion port
Expansion slot
Floppy disk
Function key
Graphics card
Graphics tablet
Hard disk
Hard disk platter
Head crash
Ink jet printer
ISA
Joystick
Keyboard shortcut
Lands
Laser printer
LCD

Magnetic storage
Milliseconds
Modem card
Modifier key
MPEG-2
Multifunction devices
Network card
Numeric keypad
Optical storage
Parallel port
PCI
PCMCIA slot
Peripheral device
Pits
Plug and Play
Printer control language (PCL)
RAID
RAM
Random access
Read-write head
Resolution
Revolutions per minute (rpm)
Scanner
Screen size

SCSI
Sequential access
Solid ink printer
Sound card
Storage capacity
Storage device
Storage medium
Storage technology
SuperDisk
Tape
Tape cartridge
TFT (thin film transistor)
Thermal transfer printer
Toggle key
Touchpad
Trackball
Track point
Ultra ATA
Viewable image size (vis)
Volatile
Windows Registry
Write-protect window
Zip disk

▼ UNIT REVIEW

1. Make sure that you can use your own words to define the bold terms that appear throughout the unit.

2. Describe the advantages and disadvantages of magnetic storage and optical storage.

3. Create a grid with each type of storage device written across the top. Make a list of the corresponding media down the left side of the grid. Working down each column, place an X in cells for any of the media that can be read by the device listed at the top of the column.

4. Summarize the most important uses for each type of storage technology.

5. Summarize display devices. Be sure to include advantages and disadvantages.

6. Create a table to summarize what you know about the printer technologies that were discussed in this unit.

7. List any peripheral devices that are attached to your computer. Describe what each one does. Be sure to identify each one as input, output, or storage.

8. If possible, open your computer and count the number of expansion slots that are not currently in use and how many are in use.

9. Look at the front of your computer and identify the devices that are in the drive bays.

10. Count the number of cables coming out of the back of your computer. Using Figure B-25, identify each type of cable.

▼ FILL IN THE BEST ANSWER

1. Data on an optical storage medium is stored as _____ and lands.

2. _____ time is the average time that it takes a computer to locate data on a storage medium and read it.

3. A computer can move directly to any file on a(n) _____ access device, but must start at the beginning and read through all of the data on a(n) _____ access device.

4. Higher disk _____ provides increased storage capacity.

5. "HD DS" means _____.

6. EIDE, Ultra ATA, and SCSI refer to the type of _____ used by a hard disk drive.

7. CD-R technology allows you to _____ data on a disk, then change that data.

8. Movie files are much too large to fit on a DVD unless they are compressed, using a special type of data coding called _____.

9. The _____ bus carries data from RAM to peripheral devices.

10. AGP, PCI, and ISA are types of expansion _____, which are part of a personal computer's motherboard.

11. Many peripheral devices come packaged with device _____ software.

12. A scanner is a type of _____ device.

13. Most people set their monitors to a(n) _____ of 640 × 480, 800 × 600, or 1024 × 768.

14. The number of colors that a monitor can display is referred to as bit _____.

15. The advantages of an LCD _____ include display clarity, low radiation emission and portability.

16. The most popular printers for personal computers are _____, which are inexpensive and produce good-quality color printouts.

17. Today's PCs include a feature called Plug and _____ that automatically takes care of technical details for installing peripheral devices.

18. A _____ key such as the [Ctrl] key is used in conjunction with other keys to expand the abilities of each key.

19. Track points and touchpads are alternative _____ devices often found on notebook computers.

20. A read-write _____ is a mechanism in the disk drive that reads and writes the magnetized particles that represent data.

▼ INDEPENDENT CHALLENGE 1

You know that you're really a tech wizard when you can decipher every term and acronym in a computer ad. But even the most knowledgeable computer gurus sometimes need a dictionary for new terms.

1. For this independent challenge, photocopy a full page from a current computer magazine that contains an ad for a computer system. On the copy of the ad, use a colored pen to circle each descriptive term and acronym.

2. On a separate sheet of paper, or using a word processor, list all of the terms that you circled and write a definition for each term. If you encounter a term that was not defined in the unit, use a computer dictionary, or refer to the Webopaedia Web site (www.webopedia.com) to locate the correct definition.

3. Prepare your list to submit to your instructor. Add a summary paragraph indicating why you would or would not purchase the computer in the ad and additional information that you need before making a decision.

▼ INDEPENDENT CHALLENGE 2

Storage technology has a fascinating history. Mankind has evolved many ways to retain and store data. From the ancient days when Egyptians were writing on papyrus to modern day holographic technologies, societies have found ways to retain more and more information in permanent and safe ways.

1. To complete this independent challenge you will research the history of storage technologies and create a timeline that shows the developments. Be sure to include such items as 78-rpm records and 8-track tapes. Your research should yield some interesting technologies and systems.

2. For each technology, list the media, the device used to retrieve the information, two significant facts about the technology, the era in which it was used or popular, and what lead to its demise or obsolescence.

3. You can create the timeline using images or just words. This is a creative project. Your best research, artistic, and communication skills come together to create this timeline.

▼ INDEPENDENT CHALLENGE 3

It is important that you are familiar with the type of computer you use daily. You may need to consult your technical resource person to help you complete this independent challenge.

1. Identify the components on your computer. What type of computer are you using? What kind of system unit do you have?

2. What peripheral devices are attached to your computer? List the name brand and model number if available.

3. Draw a sketch of your computer. Label each component and identify what it does.

▼ INDEPENDENT CHALLENGE 4

 In this unit you learned about peripheral devices. Some of these are standard peripheral devices such as monitors and printers. If your office is tight for space, you might consider purchasing a multifunction device. For this project, use your library and Web resources to research information about multifunction devices.

1. Research and find the types of multifunction devices available. Categorize them by their functions: scanners, fax, phone, copiers, color or black-and-white printing, laser or inkjet. Different manufacturers bundle different capabilities into their devices. The more features a unit has, typically, the more expensive it will be.

2. Research and find the manufacturers and model numbers for three devices you would consider buying. Write a comparison of the features, strengths, and weaknesses of each model.

▼ INDEPENDENT CHALLENGE 5

 For this project, use your library and Web resources to research information in order to compare printers.

1. Use the information in this unit as well as your own resources to create a comparative table of printers.

2. Your column heads might address these questions: What types are available? What technology is used? What is the duty cycle? What is the cost range? What is the average cost per page? Who is the market for this type of printer?

3. Provide a summary statement indicating which printer you would buy and why, based on the information in your table.

▼ INDEPENDENT CHALLENGE 6

 The Issue section of this unit focused on the potential for discarded computers and other electronic devices to become a significant environmental problem. For this independent challenge, you will write a short paper about recycling computers based on information that you gather from the Internet.

1. To begin this independent challenge, consult the Internet and use your favorite search engine to search for and find Web pages to get an in-depth overview of the issue.

2. Determine the specific aspect of the issue that you will present in your paper. You might, for example, decide to focus on the toxic materials contained in computers that end up in landfills. Or you might tackle the barriers that discourage the shipment of old computers across national borders. Whatever aspect of the issue you decide to present, make sure that you can back up your discussion with facts and references to authoritative articles and Web pages.

3. You can place citations to these pages (include the author's name, article title, date of publication, and URL) at the end of your paper as endnotes, on each page as footnotes, or along with the appropriate paragraphs using parentheses. Follow your professor's instructions for submitting your paper via e-mail or as a printed document.

▼ VISUAL WORKSHOP

If you thought a holograph was just the image of Princess Leia saying "Obi-Wan Kenobi, you are my only hope," think again. Holographic storage devices are in development as a means to respond to the growing need for large-volume data storage. Holographic technologies promise data retrieval speeds far exceeding magnetic or optical storage and capacities far beyond anything currently available. Researchers are working to make this technology an affordable reality. Figure B-28 shows a Web page from the IBM Science and Technology Center at Almaden that researches holographic technologies.

FIGURE B-28

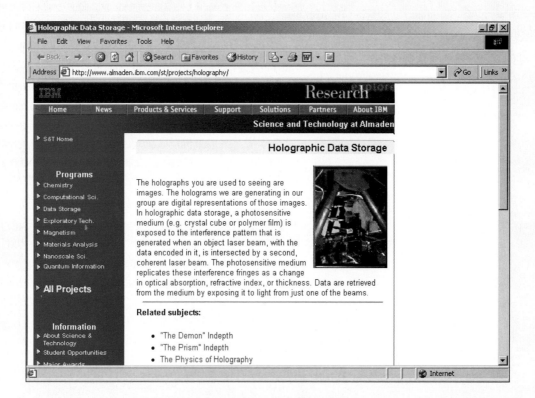

1. Use your favorite search engine to find and read the May 2000 edition of Scientific American (www.sciam.com), which included a feature article about holographic storage. Write a brief summary of the article and, based on what you read, explain the basics of how holographic memory works.

2. Research the current trends in holographic development. Are there any existing applications? How far has the technology come? What companies are working to develop these technologies? How far are we from using holocubes for data storage?

3. Write a scenario that includes the requirements and applications for holographic storage. Under what circumstances do you think such technologies would be useful, and what types of data do you think would best take advantage of this new technology?

UNIT C
Computer Software

OBJECTIVES

Introduce computer software

Explain how computers interpret software

Explore operating systems

Compare operating systems

Define document production software

Define spreadsheet software

Define data management software

Define graphics software

Define business and science software

Define entertainment and education software

Understand licenses and copyrights

Tech Talk: Install Software

A computer's versatility is possible because of software—the instructions that tell a computer how to perform a specific type of task. This unit begins with the components of a typical software package and explains how these components work together. Next, you will learn about a computer's most important system software, its operating system. You will get an overview of software applications, including document production, spreadsheets, data management, graphics, music, video editing, and games. Finally, the unit wraps up with important practical information on software copyrights and licenses and installing and uninstalling software.

Introducing computer software

In common practice, the term "software" is used to describe a commercial product. Computer software determines the types of tasks that a computer can help you accomplish. For example, some software helps you create documents, while other software helps you create presentations, prepare your tax return, or design the floor plan for a new house. You will learn about the components of computer software and how these components work together to help you complete tasks.

DETAILS

● Software is categorized as either application software or system software. **Application software** helps you carry out tasks—such as creating documents, crunching numbers, and editing photographs—using a computer. **System software**—your computer's operating system, device drivers, and utilities—helps your computer carry out its basic operating functions. Figure C-1 shows the types of software that fall into the system software and application software categories.

● **Software** consists of computer programs, support modules, and data modules that work together to provide a computer with the instructions and data necessary for carrying out a specific type of task, such as document production, video editing, or Web browsing.

● Software typically includes files that contain computer programs. A **computer program**, or "program," is a set of self-contained instructions that tells a computer how to solve a problem or carry out a task. A key characteristic of a computer program is that it can be started or "run" by a computer user. For example, the **main executable file** is a program that you run to start the software. Another file might contain the program that you use to install the software. Still another file might contain the program that you run to uninstall the software. Program files often use the .exe filename extension.

● A **support module** provides an auxiliary set of instructions that can be used in conjunction with the main software program. Each module is stored in its own file. Unlike a program file, a support module is not designed to be run by the computer user.

Instead, these modules are "called" by the computer program, as needed. For example, when you use the spelling checker in a word processing program, the word processing program calls on support modules to run the spelling checker. Support modules often use the .dll filename extension.

● A **data module** contains any data that is necessary for a task, but that is not supplied by the user. For example, word processing software checks spelling by comparing the words in a document with the words in a dictionary file. This dictionary file is a data module that is supplied by the software, not by the user.

● Most software packages include at least one executable program file, several support modules, and one or more data modules. See Figure C-2. The use of a main program file plus several support modules and data modules provides a great deal of flexibility and efficiency for programmers. For example, many of the support modules contain "generic" program instructions that can be adapted to work with a wide variety of programs. Instead of writing these instructions "from scratch," a programmer can simply plug in a generic support module.

● Most software is designed to provide a task-related environment, which includes a screen display, a means of collecting commands and data from the user, the specifications for processing data, and a method for displaying or outputting data. Figure C-3 illustrates a very simple computer program that converts a Fahrenheit temperature to Celsius and displays the result.

FIGURE C-1: Software categories

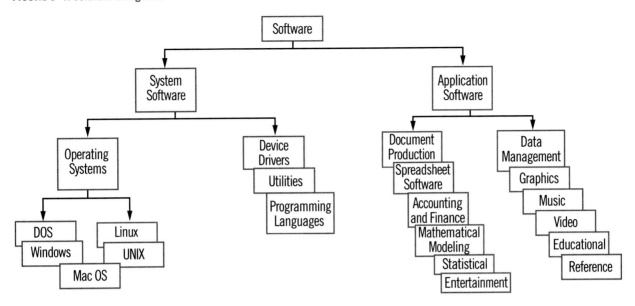

FIGURE C-2: Installed files for a software program

▶ A list of the main files required by the VideoFactory software includes program files, support modules, and data modules

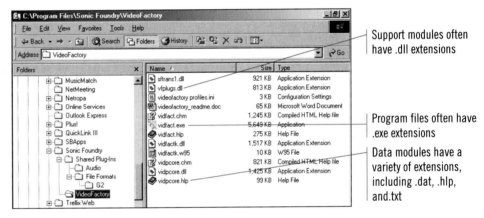

Support modules often have .dll extensions

Program files often have .exe extensions

Data modules have a variety of extensions, including .dat, .hlp, and .txt

FIGURE C-3: A simple computer program

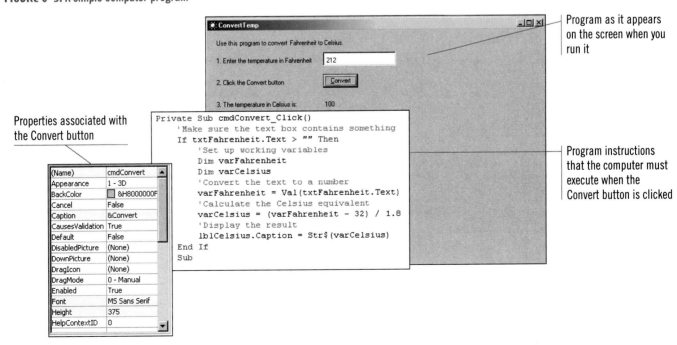

Program as it appears on the screen when you run it

Properties associated with the Convert button

Program instructions that the computer must execute when the Convert button is clicked

```
Private Sub cmdConvert_Click()
    'Make sure the text box contains something
    If txtFahrenheit.Text > "" Then
        'Set up working variables
        Dim varFahrenheit
        Dim varCelsius
        'Convert the text to a number
        varFahrenheit = Val(txtFahrenheit.Text)
        'Calculate the Celsius equivalent
        varCelsius = (varFahrenheit - 32) / 1.8
        'Display the result
        lblCelsius.Caption = Str$(varCelsius)
    End If
Sub
```

Explaining how computers interpret software

Computer programmers write the instructions for the computer programs and support modules that become the components of a computer software product. The finished software product is then distributed by the programmers themselves, or by software publishers, companies that specialize in packaging, marketing, and selling commercial software. Most businesses, organizations, and individuals purchase commercial software to avoid the time and expense of writing their own. Learning how programmers write the instructions and how a computer's microprocessor translates these instructions will help you understand how software works.

DETAILS

- A **computer language** provides the tools that a programmer uses to create software. These languages help the programmer produce a lengthy list of instructions called **source code**. Most programmers today prefer to use **high-level languages**, such as C++, Java, COBOL, and Visual Basic, which have some similarities to human languages and produce programs that are fairly easy to test and modify.

- A computer's microprocessor interprets the programmer's instructions, but the microprocessor can only understand **machine language**—the instruction set that is "hard wired" within the microprocessor's circuits. Instructions written in a high-level language must be translated into machine language before a computer can use them.

- Translating instructions from a high-level language into machine language can be accomplished by two special types of programs: compilers and interpreters. Figure C-4 gives you an idea of what happens to high-level instructions when they are converted into machine language instructions.

- A **compiler** converts high-level instructions into a new file containing machine language instructions.

A compiler translates all of the instructions in a program as a single batch, and the resulting machine language instructions, called **object code**, are placed in a new file. See Figure C-5.

- As an alternative to a compiler, an **interpreter** converts one instruction at a time while the program is running. An interpreted program runs more slowly than a compiled program because the translation process happens while the program is running. This method of converting high-level instructions into machine language is more common with Web-based programs called **scripts**, written in languages such as JavaScript and VBScript. These scripts contain high-level instructions that arrive as part of a Web page. An interpreter reads the first instruction in a script, converts it into machine language, and then sends it to the microprocessor. The interpreter continues in this way to convert instructions until all instructions are interpreted. See Figure C-6. To run a script, your computer must have the corresponding interpreter program, which is typically supplied with Web browser software or is available as a download from the Web.

FIGURE C-4: Converting a high-level instruction to machine code

High-level Language Instruction	Machine Language Equivalent	Description of Machine Language Instructions
Answer = FirstNumber + SecondNumber	10001000 00011000 010000000	Load FirstNumber into Register 1
	10001000 00010000 00100000	Load SecondNumber into Register 2
	00000000 00011000 00010000	Perform ADD operation
	10100010 00111000	Move the number from the accumulator to the RAM location called Answer

FIGURE C-5: What the compiler does

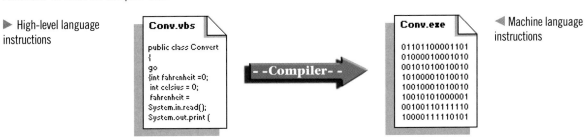

► High-level language instructions

◄ Machine language instructions

FIGURE C-6: The interpreter converts instructions one instruction at a time

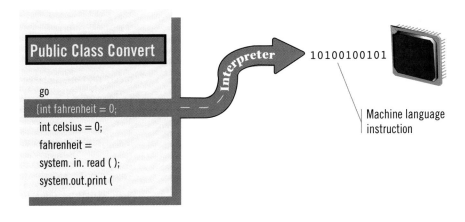

Exploring operating systems

The term **operating system** (OS) is defined as system software that acts as the master controller for all of the activities that take place within a computer system. If you understand how an operating system works, you will understand how your computer performs its many functions. For example, when you issue a command using application software, the application software tells the operating system what to do. See Figure C-7. While you interact with application software, your computer's operating system is busy behind the scenes with tasks such as identifying storage space, allocating memory, and communicating with your peripheral devices.

DETAILS

● The operating system interacts with application software, device drivers, and hardware to manage a computer's resources. For example, your operating system stores and retrieves files from your disks and CDs. It remembers the names and locations of all your files and keeps track of empty spaces where new files can be stored. It communicates with device driver software so that data can travel smoothly between the computer and the peripheral resources. If a peripheral device or driver is not performing correctly, the operating system makes a decision about what to do; usually it displays an on-screen warning about the problem.

● Many activities called "processes" compete for the attention of your computer's microprocessor. For example, commands are arriving from programs that you're using while input is arriving from the keyboard and mouse. At the same time, data must be sent to the display device or printer, and Web pages are arriving from your Internet connection. To manage all of these competing processes, your computer's operating system helps the microprocessor switch tasks. From the user's vantage point, everything seems to be happening at the same time. This is because the operating system makes sure that the microprocessor doesn't stop processing while it is waiting for instructions for a different processing task.

● When you want to multitask—run more than one program at a time—the operating system has to allocate specific areas of memory for each program. While multiple programs are running, the OS must ensure that instructions and data from one area of memory don't "leak" into an area

allocated to another program. If an OS falls down on the job and fails to protect each program's memory area, data can get corrupted, programs can "crash," and your computer will display error messages, such as "General Protection Fault." Your PC can sometimes recover from memory leak problems if you use the Ctrl-Alt-Del key sequence to close the corrupted program.

● Your computer's operating system ensures that input and output proceed in an orderly manner, using queues to collect data and buffers to hold data while the computer is busy with other tasks. By using a keyboard buffer, for example, your computer never misses one of your keystrokes, regardless of how fast you type or what else is happening within your computer system at the same time.

● Many operating systems also influence the "look and feel" of your software by determining the kinds of menus, toolbars, and controls that are displayed on the screen for all of its compatible software, and how they react to your input. Most operating systems today support a **graphical user interface**, which provides a way to point and click a mouse to select menu options and manipulate graphical objects that are displayed on the screen. See Figure C-8. Graphical user interface is sometimes abbreviated "GUI" and referred to as a "gooey."

● Although their main purpose is to control what happens "behind the scenes" of a computer system, many operating systems provide helpful tools, called **utilities**, that you can use to control and customize your computer equipment and work environment. Table C-1 lists some OS utilities.

FIGURE C-7: How the operating system interacts with the application software

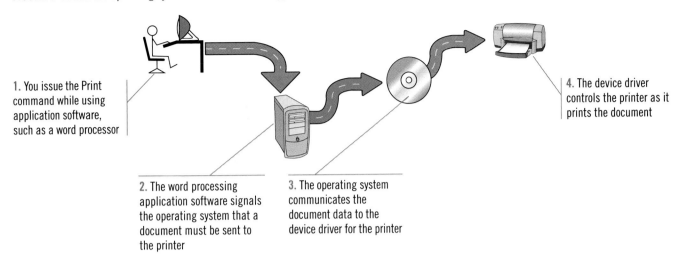

1. You issue the Print command while using application software, such as a word processor

2. The word processing application software signals the operating system that a document must be sent to the printer

3. The operating system communicates the document data to the device driver for the printer

4. The device driver controls the printer as it prints the document

FIGURE C-8: Example of a graphical user interface (GUI)

▶ A graphical user interface features menus and icons that you can manipulate with the click of a mouse

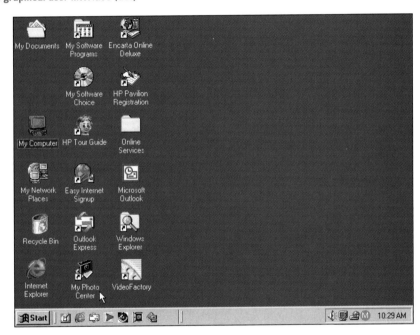

TABLE C-1: Examples of Windows operating system utilities

UTILITY USED TO	WHAT WINDOWS PROVIDES
Launch programs	When you start your computer, Windows displays a "desktop" that contains a collection of graphical objects, such as the Start menu, which you can manipulate to start programs.
Manage files	Windows Explorer allows you to view a list of files, move them to different storage devices, copy them, rename them, and delete them.
Get help	Windows provides a Help system that you can use to find out how various commands work.
Customize the user interface	The Control Panel, accessible from the Start menu, provides utilities that help you customize your screen display and work environment.
Configure equipment	The Windows Control Panel also provides access to utilities that help you set up and configure your computer's hardware and peripheral devices.

Comparing operating systems

The operating system is the master controller of your computer system. It determines how you interact with your computer. This lesson discusses categories of operating systems and compares the main features of popular operating systems.

DETAILS

- Operating systems are informally categorized using one or more of the following terms:

    A **single-user operating system** expects to deal with one set of input devices—those that can be controlled by one user at a time. Operating systems for handheld computers and many personal computers fit into the single-user category.

    A **multiuser operating system** is designed to deal with input, output, and processing requests from many users at the same time. One of its most difficult responsibilities is to schedule all of the processing requests that must be performed by a centralized computer, often a mainframe.

    A **network operating system**, or **server operating system**, provides communications and routing services that allow computers to share data, programs, and peripheral devices. While a multiuser OS and a network OS may sound the same, a multiuser operating system schedules requests for processing on a centralized computer; a network operating system simply routes data and programs to each user's local computer, where the actual processing takes place.

    A **desktop operating system** is one that's designed for either a desktop or notebook personal computer. The computer that you typically use at home, at school, or at work is most likely configured with a desktop operating system. Typically, these operating systems are designed to accommodate a single user, but may also provide networking capability.

    Today's desktop operating systems invariably provide multitasking services. A **multitasking operating system** provides process and memory management services that allow two or more programs to run simultaneously. Most of today's personal computers use operating systems that offer multitasking services.

- **Microsoft Windows** is installed on over 80 percent of the world's personal computers. Since its introduction, Windows has evolved through several versions. Windows 95, Windows 98, Windows ME, and Windows XP are classified as desktop operating systems that provide basic networking capabilities. Windows NT, Windows 2000, and Windows XP Professional are typically classified as server operating systems, because they are designed to handle the demands of medium-size to large-size networks.

- Like Windows, **Mac OS** has been through a number of revisions, including OS X (X means version 10), which made its debut in 2001.

- Both Mac OS for the Apple Macintosh computer and Windows base their user interfaces on the graphical model that was pioneered at Xerox. A quick comparison of Figure C-9 and Figure C-10 shows that both Mac and Windows interfaces use a mouse to point and click various icons and menus. Both interfaces feature rectangular work areas for multitasking services and provide basic networking services. Many of the most prolific software publishers produce one version of their software for Windows and another version for Mac OS.

- The **UNIX** operating system was developed in 1969 at AT&T's Bell Labs. It gained a good reputation for its dependability in multiuser environments. Many versions of it became available for mainframes and microcomputers.

- In 1991, a young Finnish student named Linus Torvalds developed the **Linux** operating system, based on a version of UNIX. Linux is rather unique because it is distributed under the terms of a General Public License (GPL), which allows everyone to make copies for their own use, to give it to others, or to sell it. This licensing policy has encouraged programmers to develop Linux utilities, software, and enhancements. Linux is primarily distributed over the Web.

    The Linux operating system includes such features as multitasking, TCP/IP drivers, and multiuser capabilities. These features make Linux a popular operating system for e-mail and Web servers, as well as for local area networks. Linux has been gaining popularity as a desktop operating system. See Figure C-11. Some new personal computers come configured with Linux instead of Windows or Mac OS.

- **DOS** stands for Disk Operating System. It was developed by Microsoft, the same company that later produced Windows. It was introduced on the original IBM PC in 1982. Although IBM called this operating system PC-DOS, Microsoft marketed it to other companies under the name MS-DOS. After more than 20 years, the remnants of DOS still linger as part of the operating system for Windows versions 3.1, 95, 98, and ME. Today, users rarely interact with DOS.

FIGURE C-9: Microsoft Windows

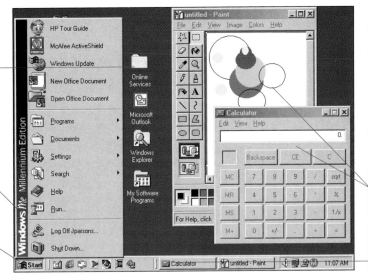

Icons represent computer hardware and software

The left side of the Start menu usually displays the version of the Windows OS that is in use

The Start button provides access to a menu of programs, documents, and utilities

◀ The Windows operating system gets its name from the rectangular work areas that appear on the screen-based desktop; each work area can display a different document or program, providing a visual model of the operating system's multitasking capabilities

Two different programs can run in two separate windows

The taskbar indicates which programs are running

FIGURE C-10: Mac OS

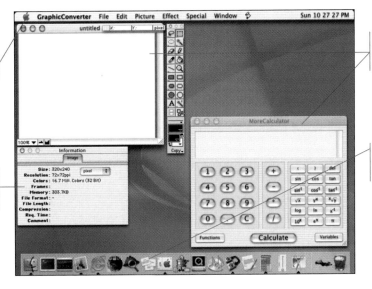

The Apple logo provides access to a menu

Menus and other on-screen objects are manipulated by using a mouse

Two different programs can run in two separate windows

Icons represent computer hardware components and software

FIGURE C-11: Linux

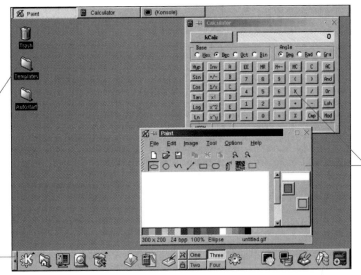

Desktop icons look similar to those on the Windows and Macintosh desktops

A horizontal option bar combines features of the Windows Start menu, Control Panel, and taskbar

◀ Linux users can choose from several graphical interfaces; this is the popular KDE (K Desktop Environment)

Two different programs can run in two separate windows

Defining document production software

Whether you are writing a 10-page paper, writing software documentation, designing a brochure for your new startup company, or laying out the school newspaper, you will probably use some form of **document production software**. This software assists you with composing, editing, designing, printing, and electronically publishing documents.

DETAILS

- Three popular types of document production software:

    Word processing software issued to produce documents such as reports, letters, and manuscripts. Word processing software gives you the ability to compose a document on the screen before you commit it to paper. Refer to Figure C-12.

    Desktop publishing software (DTP) takes word processing software one step further by helping you use graphic design techniques to enhance the format and appearance of a document. Although today's word processing software offers many page layout and design features, desktop publishing software provides more sophisticated features to help you produce professional-quality output for publications.

    Web authoring software helps you design and develop Web pages that you can publish electronically on the Internet. Web authoring software provides easy-to-use tools for composing the text for a Web page, assembling graphical elements, and automatically generating HTML tags.

- Table C-2 describes common features of document production software. None of these automated features, however, can substitute for a thorough proofreading of your document.

- The **format** for a document refers to how all text, pictures, titles, and page numbers are arranged on the page. The look of your document will depend on formatting factors, such as font style, paragraph style (see Figure C-13), and page layout.

- **Page layout** refers to the physical position of each element on a page. A **header** is text that you specify to appear in the top margin of every page automatically. A **footer** is text that you specify to appear in the bottom margin of every page automatically. **Clip art** is a collection of drawings and photos designed to be inserted into documents. A **table** is a grid-like structure that can hold text or pictures. For printed documents, tables are a popular way to provide easy-to-read columns of data and to position graphics. For Web pages, tables provide one of the few ways to position text and pictures precisely.

- Frame-oriented software allows you to divide each page into several rectangular-shaped **frames** that you can fill with either text or pictures. See Figure C-14. Frames provide you with finer control over the position of elements on a page, such as a figure and a caption on top of it. DTP software is usually frame oriented.

TABLE C-2: Some features of document production software

FEATURE	DESCRIPTION
alignment	determines position of text as left, right, centered, or full justified
autocorrect	automatically changes a typo, such as "teh" to "the"
find and replace	finds all occurrences of a word or phrase and lets you replace it with another word or phrase, such as changing May to August
formatting options	allows you change font, font size, font style
line spacing	determines the space between lines of type, such as single space
mail merge	creates personalized letters by automatically combining information in a mailing list with a form letter
spelling checker/ grammar checker	marks words in a document as misspelled if they do not match words in the spelling dictionary; reads through your document and points out potential grammatical trouble spots, such as run-on sentences
style	saved set of formatting options that you apply to text; you can create character, paragraph, table, and list styles

FIGURE C-12: Microsoft Word

As you type, the spelling checker compares your words with a list of correctly spelled words; words not included in the list are marked with a wavy line as possible misspellings

Even after you type an entire document, adjusting the size of your right, left, top, and bottom margins is simple

Document production software uses word wrap automatically to fit your text within the margins

Proper nouns and scientific, medical, and technical words are likely to be flagged as misspelled even if you spell them correctly because they do not appear in the spelling checker's dictionary

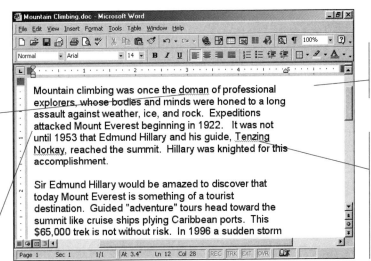

FIGURE C-13: Applying a style

The style called Document title specifies Times New Roman font, size 18, bold, and centered

Paragraph alignment buttons

Applying the formats assigned to a style simply requires you to highlight the text, then click a style from the list, such as the Document title style

FIGURE C-14: Using frames

One frame holds the centered title and author's byline

A frame can be positioned anywhere on the page—even in the center of two text columns

Wrapping text around a frame adds interest to the layout

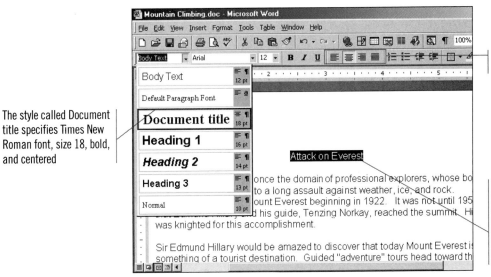

Attack on Everest
by Janell Chalmers

Mountain climbing was once the domain of professional explorers, whose bodies and minds were honed to a long assault against weather, ice, and rock. Expeditions attacked Mount Everest beginning in 1922. It was not until 1953 that Edmund Hillary and his guide, Tenzing Norkay, reached the summit. Hillary was knighted for this accomplishment.

Sir Edmund Hillary would be amazed to discover that today Mount Everest is something of a tourist destination. Guided "adventure" tours head toward the

summit like cruise ships plying Caribbean ports. This $65,000 trek is not without risk. In 1996 a sudden storm killed eight climbers.

Back in 1923, British mountaineer, George Mallory was asked, why climb Everest? His reply, "Because it's there." A new answer to this question, "Because we can" may be largely attributable to new high-tech mountain gear. Nylon, polypropylene and Gore-Tex clothing provide light, yet warm protection from the elements. Ultraviolet lenses protect eyes from dangerous "snow-blindness."

"Because it's there."
George Mallory

Graphical elements such as photos, diagrams, graphs, and pie charts can be incorporated in your documents using frames

Defining spreadsheet software

Spreadsheet software, used for numerical calculations, was initially popular with accountants and financial managers who dealt with paper-based spreadsheets, but found the electronic version far easier to use and less prone to errors than manual calculations. Other people soon discovered the benefits of spreadsheets for projects that require repetitive calculations: budgeting, maintaining a grade book, balancing a checkbook, tracking investments, calculating loan payments, and estimating project costs. You can use spreadsheets to make other calculations too, based on simple equations or more complex formulas. Spreadsheet software can turn your data into a variety of colorful graphs and charts.

DETAILS

● A **spreadsheet** uses rows and columns of numbers to create a model or representation of a real situation. For example, your checkbook register is a type of spreadsheet because it is a numerical representation of the cash flowing in and out of your bank account. **Spreadsheet software** provides tools to create electronic spreadsheets.

● You use spreadsheet software to create an on-screen **worksheet** like the one shown in Figure C-15. A worksheet is based on a grid of columns and rows. Each **cell** in the grid can contain a value, label, or formula and has a unique **cell reference**, or "address," derived from its column and row location. For example, A1 is the cell reference for the upper-left cell in a worksheet because it is in column A and row 1. You can select any cell and make it the active cell by clicking it. Once a cell is active, you can enter data into it. A **value** is a number that you want to use in a calculation. A **label** is any text that is used to describe data.

● The values contained in a cell can be manipulated by formulas that are placed in other cells. A **formula** works behind the scenes to tell the computer how to use the contents of cells in calculations. You can enter a simple formula in a cell to add, subtract, multiply, or divide numbers. Figure C-16 illustrates how a formula might be used in a simple spreadsheet to calculate savings. More complex formulas can be designed to perform just about any calculation you can imagine. You can enter a formula "from scratch" by typing it into a cell, or you can use a

function, which is a predefined formula built into the spreadsheet software.

● Unless you specify otherwise, a cell reference is a **relative reference**—a reference that can change if cells are deleted or inserted and the data or a formula moves. See Figure C-17. If you don't want a cell reference to change, you can use an absolute reference. An **absolute reference** never changes when you delete or insert cells or copy or move formulas. Understanding when to use absolute references is one of the key aspects to developing spreadsheet design expertise.

● When you change the contents of any cell in a worksheet, all of the formulas are recalculated. This **automatic recalculation** feature assures you that the results in every cell are accurate with regard to the information currently entered in the worksheet. Your worksheet is also automatically updated to reflect any rows or columns that you add, delete, or copy within the worksheet.

● Most spreadsheet software includes a few templates or wizards for predesigned worksheets, such as invoices, income-expense reports, balance sheets, and loan payment schedules. Additional templates are available on the Web. These templates are typically designed by content professionals and contain all of the necessary labels and formulas. To use a template, you simply plug in the values for your calculation.

FYI

Spreadsheet software is useful for what-if analyses, such as, "Is it better to take out a 30-year mortgage at 8.5% interest or a 15-year mortgage at 7.75% interest?"

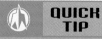

QUICK TIP

You can format the labels and values on a worksheet by changing fonts and font size, selecting a font color, and selecting a font style, such as bold.

FIGURE C-15: An on-screen worksheet

Each column is lettered
Cell A1
Each row is numbered
Values in these cells can be used for calculations
Labels, such as Profit and Expenses, identify data

The active cell is indicated by a black border
A formula in this cell subtracts the Expenses from the Income to calculate Profit

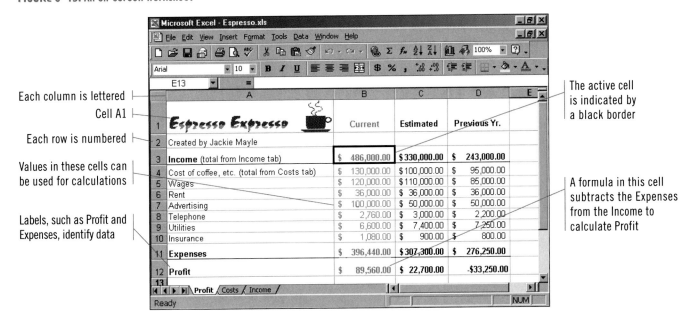

FIGURE C-16: How formulas work

► When a cell contains a formula, it displays the result of the formula, rather than the formula itself

The number that appears in cell B6 was calculated by the spreadsheet based on the formula typed in the cell

The formula for cell B6 is shown on the Formula bar

FIGURE C-17: Relative vs. absolute references

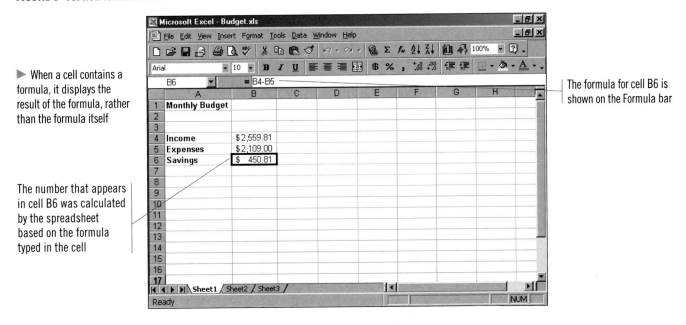

Two blank rows

The original formula =B4-B5 uses relative references

When row 3 is deleted, the Income and Expenses values move up one row, which means that these values have new cell references; the formula changes to =B3-B4 to reflect the new cell references

► Relative references within a formula can change when you insert or delete rows and columns or when you copy or move formulas; an absolute reference is "anchored" so that it always refers to a specific cell

Defining data management software

Data management software helps you to store, find, organize, update, and report information. Several types of data management software exist, including file management software and database management software. This lesson provides background on structured files and the file management software designed for these files, as well as a discussion of databases and the database management software designed for databases.

Info Web

DATA MANAGEMENT
SOFTWARE

DETAILS

● A **structured file** is a collection of records, each with the same set of fields that can hold data. Each **record** holds data for a single entity—a person, place, thing, or event. A **field** holds one item of data relevant to a record. Figure C-18 illustrates records and fields in a structured file. A single file, sometimes called a **flat file**, can be a useful repository for simple lists of information, such as e-mail addresses, holiday card addresses, doctor visits, appointments, or household valuables.

● **File management software** is designed to help you create, modify, search, sort, and print simple lists, or flat files. Some file management software is tailored to special applications. A **personal information manager**, for example, is a specialized file system that keeps track of daily appointments, addresses, and To Do lists.

● In contrast to a single flat file, a **database** is a collection of files that can be treated as a single unit, sometimes referred to as a table. For example, suppose you have one computer file containing video information and another containing information about performers. Database software lets you join the two files together to display the information about the video and performers at the same time.

   Most of today's databases are based on either a relational model or an object-oriented model. A **relational database** structures each file as a table in which each column is a field and each

row is a record. Relationships can be established between tables to join the tables together so that they can be treated as one, as shown in Figure C-19. An **object-oriented database** treats each record as a unit that can be manipulated using program instructions called methods. For example, a university database containing information about its students might include an object called "Course Grades" and a method called "Calculate GPA."

● **Database management software** (DBMS) is designed for creating and manipulating the multiple files that form a database. Most of today's database management software is designed for creating and manipulating relational databases. Special object-oriented database management software is required for creating and manipulating object-oriented databases.

● Your data management software, whether it is file management software or database management software, requires you to create a file structure. A **file structure** is somewhat like a fill-in form that contains a list of fields and their data types that define the data in the file. See Figure C-20. Once you create a file structure, you can enter the data for each of your records. With the data in place, you can modify the data in individual records to keep it up to date. Your data management software also will help you print reports, export data to other programs (such as to a spreadsheet, where you can graph the data), convert the data to other formats (such as HTML, so that you can post the data on the Web), and transmit data to other computers.

Searching flat files and databases

Many flat files and databases contain hundreds or thousands of records. If you want to find a particular record or a group of records, scrolling through every record is much too cumbersome. Instead, you can enter search specifications called a **query**, and the computer will quickly locate the records you seek. Most data management software provides one or more methods for making queries. A **query language** provides a set of commands for locating and manipulating data. **SQL** (Structured Query Language) is a popular query language used by numerous data

management software packages. In addition to a formal query language, some data management software provides **natural language query** capabilities. To make such queries, you don't have to learn an esoteric query language. Instead, you can simply enter questions using natural language. As an alternative to a query language or a natural language query, your data management software might allow you to **query by example** (QBE), simply by filling out a form with the type of data that you want to locate.

FIGURE C-18: A structured file

▶ In a file of library books, data for each book is stored as a record in the file; the record for each book contains a standard set of fields with data that pertains to the book

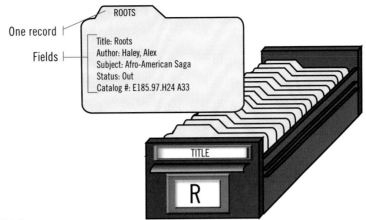

One record

ROOTS

Fields

Title: Roots
Author: Haley, Alex
Subject: Afro-American Saga
Status: Out
Catalog #: E185.97.H24 A33

TITLE

R

FIGURE C-19: A relational database

▶ A relational database can contain multiple files, which are represented by tables; equivalent fields in each table can be used to join the records in these tables so that you can see the data in both tables at the same time

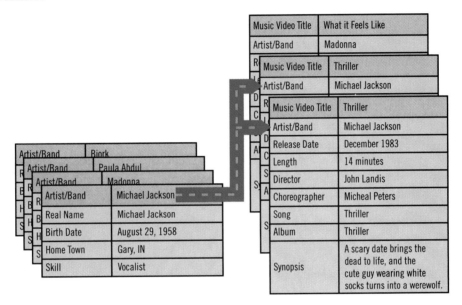

Music Video Title	What it Feels Like
Artist/Band	Madonna

Music Video Title	Thriller
Artist/Band	Michael Jackson

Music Video Title	Thriller
Artist/Band	Michael Jackson
Release Date	December 1983
Length	14 minutes
Director	John Landis
Choreographer	Micheal Peters
Song	Thriller
Album	Thriller
Synopsis	A scary date brings the dead to life, and the cute guy wearing white socks turns into a werewolf.

Artist/Band	Bjork
Artist/Band	Paula Abdul

Artist/Band	Madonna
Artist/Band	Michael Jackson
Real Name	Michael Jackson
Birth Date	August 29, 1958
Home Town	Gary, IN
Skill	Vocalist

FIGURE C-20: Database management software

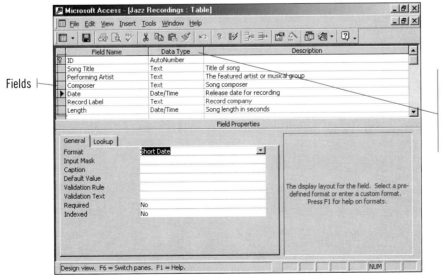

Fields

When you define a field, you can specify its data type as either character data, numeric data, date data, logical data, hyperlink data, or memo data

Defining graphics software

In computer lingo, the term **graphics** refers to any picture, drawing, sketch, photograph, image, or icon that appears on your computer screen. **Graphics software** is designed to help you create, display, modify, manipulate, and print graphics. Many kinds of graphics software exist, and each one typically specializes in a particular type of graphic. If you are really interested in working with graphics, you will undoubtedly end up using more than one graphics software package.

DETAILS

● **Paint software** (sometimes called "image editing software") provides a set of electronic pens, brushes, and paints for painting images on the screen. Graphic artists, Web page designers, photographers, and illustrators use paint software as their primary computer-based graphics tool.

● **Photo editing software** includes features specially designed to fix poor-quality photos by modifying contrast and brightness, cropping out unwanted objects, and removing "red eye." Photos can also be edited using paint software, but photo editing software typically provides tools and wizards that simplify common photo editing tasks.

● **Drawing software** provides a set of lines, shapes, and colors that can be assembled into diagrams, corporate logos, and schematics. The drawings created with this type of software tend to have a "flat" cartoon-like quality, but they are very easy to modify and look good at just about any size. Figure C-21 provides more information on paint, photo editing, and drawing software.

● **3-D graphics software** provides a set of tools for creating "wireframes" that represent three-dimensional objects. A wireframe acts much like the framework for a pop-up tent. Just as you would construct the framework for the tent, then cover it with a nylon tent cover, 3-D graphics software can cover a wireframe object with surface texture and color to create a graphic of a 3-D object. See Figure C-22.

● **CAD software** (computer-aided design software) is a special type of 3-D graphics software designed for architects and engineers who use computers to create blueprints and product specifications. Scaled-down versions of professional CAD software provide simplified tools for homeowners who want to redesign their kitchens, examine new landscaping options, or experiment with floor plans.

● **Presentation software** provides all of the tools you need for combining text, graphics, graphs, animations, and sound into a series of electronic **slides.** You can display the electronic slides on a color monitor for a one-on-one presentation or use a computer projection device, like the one shown in Figure C-23, for group presentations. You can also output the presentation as overhead transparencies, paper copies, or 35-mm slides.

FIGURE C-21: Images created using paint, photo editing, and drawing software

▲ Paint software works well with realistic art and photos

▲ Photo editing software includes special features for touching up photographs

▲ Drawing software tends to create two-dimensional "cartoon-like" images

FIGURE C-22: 3-D graphics tools

▶ Some 3-D software specializes in drawing figures

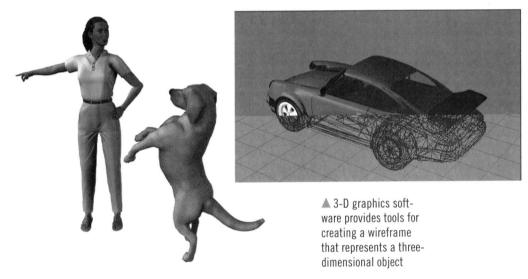

▲ 3-D graphics software provides tools for creating a wireframe that represents a three-dimensional object

FIGURE C-23: A computer-based presentation

▲ A presentation can be displayed for a group by using a projection device

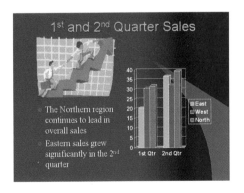

▲ A computer-based presentation consists of a series of slides that can include graphics, bulleted lists, and charts

UNIT C

Defining business and science software

The terms business software and science software provide a broad umbrella for several types of software that are designed to help businesses and organizations accomplish routine or specialized tasks. These types of software provide a structured environment dedicated to a particular number-crunching task, such as money management, mathematical modeling, or statistical analysis.

DETAILS

- **Accounting and finance software** helps you keep a record of monetary transactions and investments. In this software category, **personal finance software** (Figure C-24) is geared toward individual finances. **Tax preparation software** is a specialized type of personal finance software designed to help you gather your annual income and expense data, identify deductions, and calculate your tax payment.

- Some accounting and finance software is geared toward business. If you're an entrepreneur, **small business accounting software** can be a real asset. These easy-to-use programs don't require more than a basic understanding of accounting and finance principles. This type of software helps you invoice customers and keep track of what they owe. It stores additional customer data, such as contact information and purchasing history. Inventory functions keep track of the products that you carry. Payroll capabilities automatically calculate wages and deduct federal, state, and local taxes.

- **Vertical market software** is designed to automate specialized tasks in a specific market or business. Examples include patient management and billing software specially designed for hospitals, job estimating software for construction businesses, and student record management software for schools. Today, almost every business has access to some type of specialized vertical market software designed to automate, streamline, or computerize key business activities.

- **Horizontal market software** is generic software that can be used by just about any kind of business. **Payroll software** is a good example of horizontal market software. Almost every business has employees and must maintain payroll records. No

matter what type of business uses it, payroll software must collect similar data and make similar calculations in order to produce payroll checks and W2 forms. Accounting software and project management software are additional examples of horizontal market software. **Accounting software** helps a business keep track of the money flowing in and out of various accounts. **Project management software** is an important tool for planning large projects, scheduling project tasks, and tracking project costs.

- **Groupware**, another umbrella term in the world of business software, is designed to help several people collaborate on a single project using network or Internet connections. It usually provides the capability to maintain schedules for all of the group members, automatically select meeting times for the group, facilitate communication by e-mail or other channels, distribute documents according to a prearranged schedule or sequence, and allow multiple people to contribute to a single document.

- One type of science-related software is **statistical software**, which helps you analyze large sets of data to discover relationships and patterns. It is a helpful tool for summarizing survey results, test scores, experiment results, or population data. Most statistical software includes graphing capability so that you can display and explore your data visually.

- **Mathematical modeling software**, such as MathCAD and Mathematica, provides tools for solving a wide range of math, science, and engineering problems. See Figure C-25. Students, teachers, mathematicians, and engineers, in particular, appreciate how this software helps them recognize patterns that can be difficult to identify in columns of numbers.

FIGURE C-24: Personal finance software

▶ Personal finance software helps you keep track of bank accounts, investments, credit card balances, and bills; some packages also support online banking, a way to use your computer and modem to download transactions directly from your bank, transfer funds between accounts, and pay bills

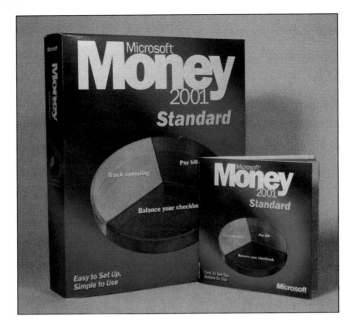

FIGURE C-25: Visualization of equation using mathematics software

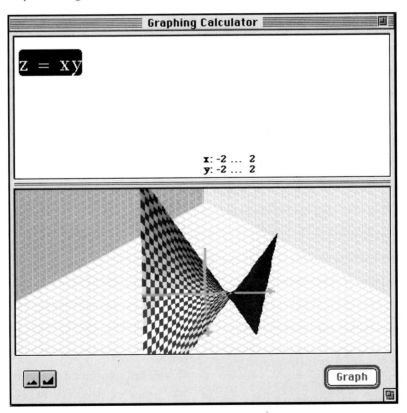

Why spreadsheet software is not always the best software for businesses

Spreadsheet software provides a tool to work with numeric models by using values, labels, and formulas. The advantage of spreadsheet software is its flexibility. You can create customized calculations according to your exact specifications. The disadvantage of spreadsheet software is that, aside from a few pre-designed templates, you are responsible for entering formulas and selecting functions for calculations. If you don't know the formulas, or don't understand the functions, you would do much better to purchase a business software package with those functions to meet your specific needs.

Defining entertainment and education software

The computer can provide entertainment in many formats, including listening to music, watching videos, and playing games. Computer games are the most popular type of entertainment software. Over $6 billion of computer and video games are sold each year in the U.S. Software classified as educational can also be entertaining; these software categories often overlap.

DETAILS

● It is easy to make your own digital voice and music recordings and store them on your computer's hard disk. Windows and Mac OS operating system utilities typically supply the necessary **audio editing software**, including Sound Recorder on PCs (see Figure C-26), and iTunes on iMacs. Audio editing software typically includes playback as well as recording capabilities. A specialized version of this software called Karaoke software integrates music files and on-screen lyrics; everything you need to sing along with your favorite tunes.

● **MP3** is a music compression file format that stores digitized music in such a way that the sound quality is excellent, but the file size remains relatively small—small enough to be easily downloaded from the Web. To listen to MP3 music on your computer, you need an **MP3 player**. Versions of MP3 player software are available for many handheld computers and for personal computers running Windows, Mac OS, and Linux.

● **Ear training software** targets musicians and music students who want to learn to play by ear, develop tuning skills, recognize notes and keys, and develop other musical skills. **Notation software** is the musician's equivalent of a word processor. It helps musicians compose, edit, and print the notes for their compositions. For non-musicians, **computer-aided music software** is designed to generate unique musical compositions simply by selecting the musical style, instruments, key, and tempo. **MIDI sequencing software** and software synthesizers are an important part of the studio musician's toolbox. They're great for sound effects and for controlling keyboards and other digital instruments.

● The growing popularity of computer-based video editing can be attributed to video editing software, such as Windows Movie Maker and Apple iMovie, now included with Windows computers and iMacs. **Video editing software** provides a set of tools for transferring video footage from a camcorder to a computer, clipping out unwanted footage, assembling video segments in any sequence, adding special visual effects, and adding a sound track. Despite an impressive array of features, video editing software is relatively easy to use, as explained in Figure C-27.

● Computer games are generally classified into subcategories, such as role-playing, action, adventure, puzzles, simulations, and strategy/war games. Since it was established in 1994, the Entertainment Software Rating Board (ESRB) has rated more than 7,000 video and computer games. Rating symbols, shown in Figure C-28, can usually be found on the game box.

● **Educational software** helps you learn and practice new skills. For the youngest students, educational software, such as MindTwister Math and 3-D Froggy Phonics, teaches basic arithmetic and reading skills. Instruction is presented in game format, and the levels of play are adapted to the player's age and ability. For older students and adults, software is available for such diverse educational endeavors as learning languages, training yourself to use new software, learning how to play the piano or guitar, preparing for standardized tests, improving keyboarding skills, and even learning managerial skills for a diverse workplace. Exam preparation software is available for standardized tests such as the SAT, GMAT, and LSAT.

● **Reference software** provides you with a collection of information and a way to access that information. The reference software category spans a wide range of applications from encyclopedias to medical references, from map software to trip planners, and from cookbooks to telephone books. The options are as broad as the full range of human interests. Reference software is generally shipped on a CD-ROM because of the quantity of data it includes. Many of these products provide links to Web sites that contain updates for the information on the CD-ROM. Other software publishers have eliminated the CD-ROM entirely and have placed all of their reference materials on the Web. Access to that information often requires a fee or a subscription.

FIGURE C-26: Music editing software

Menus provide additional digital editing features, such as speed control, volume adjustments, clipping, and mixing

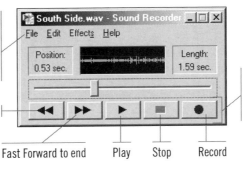

Audio editing software, such as Sound Recorder, provides controls much like a tape recorder

Rewind to beginning

Fast Forward to end   Play   Stop   Record

FIGURE C-27: Video editing software

▶ Video editing software, such as Adobe Premiere, helps you import a series of video clips from a camera or VCR, arrange the clips in the order of your choice, add transitions between clips, and add an audio track

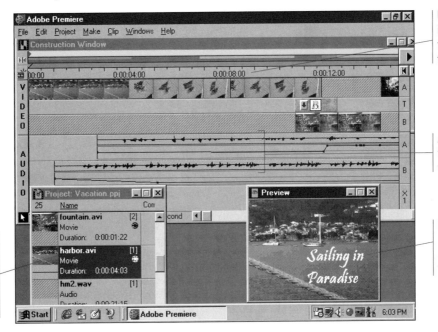

Use the timeline to indicate the sequence for your video clips and transitions

Arrange the audio tracks to synchronize with each video clip

The video and sound clips that you import for the project are displayed in a list so that you can easily select them in sequence

Preview your video to see how the clips, transitions, and soundtrack all work together

FIGURE C-28: ESRB ratings

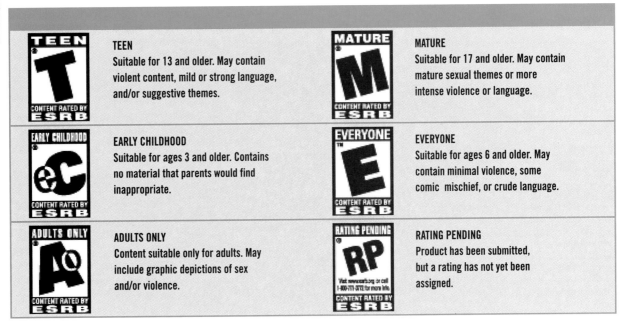

TEEN
Suitable for 13 and older. May contain violent content, mild or strong language, and/or suggestive themes.

MATURE
Suitable for 17 and older. May contain mature sexual themes or more intense violence or language.

EARLY CHILDHOOD
Suitable for ages 3 and older. Contains no material that parents would find inappropriate.

EVERYONE
Suitable for ages 6 and older. May contain minimal violence, some comic mischief, or crude language.

ADULTS ONLY
Content suitable only for adults. May include graphic depictions of sex and/or violence.

RATING PENDING
Product has been submitted, but a rating has not yet been assigned.

UNIT C

Understanding licenses and copyrights

Once you purchase a software package, you might assume that you can install it and use it in any way that you like. In fact, your "purchase" entitles you to use the software only in certain prescribed ways. In most countries, computer software, like a book or movie, is protected by a copyright. In addition to copyright protection, computer software is often protected by the terms of a software license. Copyright laws provide fairly severe restrictions on copying, distributing, and reselling software. However, a license agreement may offer some rights to consumers as well. The licenses for commercial software, shareware, freeware, open source, and public domain software provide different levels of permission for software use, copying, and distribution.

DETAILS

- A **software license**, or "license agreement," is a legal contract that defines the ways in which you may use a computer program. For personal computer software, you will find the license on the outside of the package, on a separate card inside the package, on the CD packaging, or in one of the program files.

- A **copyright** is a form of legal protection that grants the author of an original work an exclusive right to copy, distribute, sell, and modify that work, except under special circumstances described by copyright laws. Exceptions include the purchaser's right to copy software from a distribution disk or Web site to a computer's hard disk in order to install it; to make an extra, or backup, copy of the software in case the original copy becomes erased or damaged; and to copy and distribute sections of a software program for use in critical reviews and teaching.

- Most software displays a **copyright notice**, such as "© 2002 eCourseWare," on one of its screens. However, because this notice is not required by law, programs without a copyright notice are still protected by copyright law. People who circumvent copyright law and illegally copy, distribute, or modify software are sometimes called software pirates, and their illegal copies are referred to as pirated software.

- Most legal contracts require signatures before the terms of the contract take effect. This requirement becomes unwieldy with software; imagine having to sign a license agreement and return it before you can use a new software package. To circumvent the signature requirement, software publishers typically use two techniques to validate a software license: shrink-wrap licenses and

installation agreements. When you purchase computer software, the distribution disks, CDs, or DVDs are usually sealed in an envelope, plastic box, or shrink wrapping. A **shrink-wrap license** goes into effect as soon as you open the packaging. Figure C-29 explains more about the mechanics of a shrink-wrap license.

- An **installation agreement** is displayed on the screen when you first install the software. After reading the software license on the screen, you can indicate that you accept the terms of the license by clicking a designated button usually labeled "OK," "I agree," or "I accept."

- Software licenses are often lengthy and written in legalese, but your legal right to use the software continues only as long as you abide by the terms of the software license. Therefore, you should understand the software license for any software you use. When you read a software license agreement, look for answers to the following questions:

  - Am I buying the software or licensing it?
  - When does the license go into effect?
  - Under what circumstances can I make copies?
  - Can I rent the software?
  - Can I sell the software?
  - What if the software includes a distribution CD and a set of distribution disks?
  - Does the software publisher provide a warranty?
  - Can I loan the software to a friend?

FIGURE C-29: A shrink-wrap license

▶ When software has a shrink-wrap license, you agree to the terms of the software license by opening the package; if you do not agree with the terms, you should return the software in its unopened package

Examining copyright protections for software

Commercial software is typically sold in computer stores or at Web sites. Although you buy this software, you actually purchase only the right to use it under the terms of the software license. A license for commercial software typically adheres closely to the limitations provided by copyright law, although it might give you permission to install the software on a computer at work and on a computer at home, provided that you use only one of them at a time.

Shareware is copyrighted software marketed under a try before you buy policy. It typically includes a license that permits you to use the software for a trial period. To use it beyond the trial period, you must send in a registration fee. A shareware license usually allows you to make copies of the software and distribute them to others. If they choose to use the software, they must send in a registration fee as well. These shared copies provide a low-cost marketing and distribution channel.

Registration fee payment relies on the honor system, so unfortunately many shareware authors collect only a fraction of the money they deserve for their programming efforts. Thousands of shareware programs are available, encompassing just about as many applications as commercial software.

Freeware is copyrighted software that is available without a fee. Because the software is protected by copyright, you cannot do anything with it that is not expressly allowed by copyright law or by the author. Typically, the license for freeware permits you to use the software, copy it, and give it away, but does not permit you to alter it or sell it. Many utility programs, device drivers, and some games are available as freeware.

Open source software makes the uncompiled program instructions available to programmers who want to modify and improve the software. Open source software may be sold or distributed free of charge, but it must, in every case, include the uncompiled "source code." Linux is an example of open source software, as is FreeBSD—a version of UNIX designed for personal computers.

Public domain software is not protected by copyright because the copyright has expired or the author has placed the program in the public domain, making it available without restriction. Public domain software may be freely copied, distributed, and even resold. The primary restriction on public domain software is that you are not allowed to apply for a copyright on it.

Installing Software

No matter how you obtain a new software package, you must install it on your computer before you can use it. From time to time, you might also want to uninstall some of the software that exists on your computer. This Tech Talk looks at the process of installing and uninstalling software.

The ingredients necessary to install new software are the files that contain the programs, support modules, and data modules. These files might be supplied on **distribution disks**, one or more CDs, or a series of floppy disks that are packaged in a box, along with an instruction manual. Software downloaded over the Internet typically arrives as one huge file that contains the program modules and the text of the instruction manual.

Printed on the software package, or tucked away at the software publisher's Web site, you'll find a set of **system requirements**, which specifies the operating system and minimum hardware capacities for a software product to work correctly.

When you **install** software, the new software files are placed in the appropriate folders on your computer's hard disk, and then your computer performs any software or hardware configurations necessary to make sure the program is ready to run. The installation process usually includes the following activities:

- Copy files from distribution disks to specified folders on the hard disk

- Uncompress files if they have been distributed in a compressed format, such as WinZip

- Analyze the computer's resources, such as processor speed, RAM capacity, and hard disk capacity, to verify that they meet or exceed the minimum system requirements

- Analyze hardware components and peripheral devices to select appropriate device drivers

- Look for any system files and players, such as Windows Media Player or Internet Explorer, that are required to run the program but are not supplied on the distribution disks

- Update necessary system files, such as the Windows Registry and the Windows Program menu, with information about the new software

With Windows and other operating systems, application software programs share some common files. These files are often supplied by the operating system and perform routine tasks, such as displaying the Print dialog box that allows you to select a printer and specify how many copies of a file you want to print. These "shared" files are not typically provided on the distribution disks for a new software program because the files should already exist on your computer. The installation routine attempts to locate these files and will notify you if any of them are missing.

As part of the installation process, you will be asked to specify the folder that will hold the files for the new software. The main executable files and data modules for the software will be placed in the folder you specify.

Installing downloaded software

Downloaded software is usually one of the following compressed file types: self-installing executable file, self-executing zip files, or zipped files. The self-installing executable file automatically unzips itself and starts the setup program. Simply follow the setup program prompts to acknowledge the license agreement, indicate the folder for the software files, and complete the installation. A self-executing zip file automatically unzips the software's files, but does not automatically start the setup program. Under this installation system, you start the executable file to unzip the files for the new software. One of these files will be the Setup.exe program. Next, you manually start the setup program and follow its prompts to complete the installation. A zip file must be opened with a program such as WinZip. You then must run the setup program to acknowledge the license agreement, indicate the folder for the software files, and complete the installation.

Installation procedures vary depending on a computer's operating system. Windows software typically contains a **setup program** that guides you through the installation process. Figure C-30 shows you what to expect when you use a setup program.

Operating systems, such as Windows and Mac OS, provide access to an **uninstall routine** that deletes the software's files from various directories on your computer's hard disk. The uninstall routine also removes references to the program from the desktop and from operating system files, such as the file system and, in the case of Windows, from the Windows Registry. With Windows software, you can typically find the uninstall routine on the same menu as the program. If an uninstall routine is not provided by the software, you can use the one provided by the operating system. In Windows, the Add/Remove Programs icon is located in the Control Panel, accessible from the Start menu.

FIGURE C-30: Installing software from a distribution CD

1. Insert the distribution disk, CD, or DVD. The setup program should start automatically. If it does not, look for a file called *Setup.exe* and then run it.

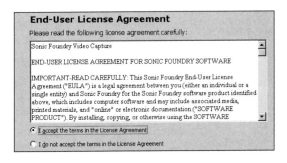

2. Read the license agreement, if one is presented on the screen. By agreeing to the terms of the license, you can proceed with the installation.

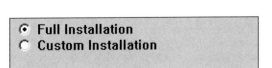

3. Select the installation option that best meets your needs. If you select a full installation, the setup program copies all files and data from the distribution medium to the hard disk of your computer system. A full installation provides you with access to all features of the software.

If you select a custom installation, the setup program displays a list of software features for your selection. After you select the features you want, the setup program copies only the selected program files, support modules, and data modules to your hard disk. A custom installation can save space on your hard disk.

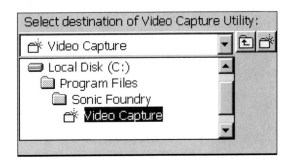

4. Follow the prompts provided by the setup program to specify a folder to hold the new software program. You can typically create a new folder during the setup process if you did not prepare a folder ahead of time.

5. If the software includes multiple distribution disks, insert each one in the specified drive when the setup program tells you to do so.

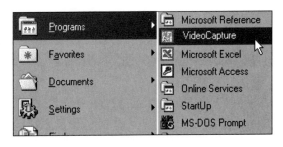

6. When the setup is complete, start the program that you just installed to make sure it works.

Issue   Is Piracy a Problem?

Software is easy to steal. You don't have to walk out of a CompUSA store with a Microsoft Office XP box under your shirt. You can simply borrow your friend's CD-ROM and install a copy of the program on your computer's hard disk. It seems so simple that it couldn't be illegal. But it is.

In many countries, including the United States, software pirates are subject to criminal prosecution. And yet, piracy continues to grow. According to the Software and Information Industry Association (SIIA), a leading anti-piracy watchdog, revenue losses from business software piracy typically exceed $12 billion per year. This figure reveals only a part of the piracy problem; it does not include losses from rampant game and educational software piracy.

A small but vocal minority of software users, such as members of GNU (which stands for "Gnu's Not UNIX"), believe that data and software should be freely distributed. Richard Stallman writes in the GNU Manifesto, "I consider that the golden rule requires that if I like a program I must share it with other people who like it. Software sellers want to divide users and conquer them, making each user agree not to share with others. I refuse to break solidarity with other users in this way. I cannot in good conscience sign a nondisclosure agreement or a software license agreement."

Is software piracy really damaging? Who cares if you use Microsoft Office without paying for it? As a consumer you should care if someone is using software they didn't pay for. Software piracy is damaging because it has a negative effect on the economy. Software production is the third largest industry in the United States, employing more than 2 million people and growing at a phenomenal rate of 5.8 percent per year. This industry, however, is losing an estimated $32 million every day, which translates to over 130,000 lost jobs and billions in lost tax revenues annually.

Decreases in software revenues can have a direct effect on consumers too. When software publishers must cut corners, they tend to reduce customer service and technical support. As a result, you, the consumer, get put on hold when you call for technical support, you find fewer free technical support sites, and you encounter customer support personnel who are only moderately knowledgeable about their products. The bottom line is that software piracy negatively affects customer service.

As an alternative to cutting support costs, some software publishers might build the cost of software piracy into the price of the software. The unfortunate result is that those who legitimately license and purchase software pay an inflated price.

Software piracy is a global problem. Although the United States accounts for the highest dollar amount of software piracy, approximately two-thirds of the piracy occurs outside the United States. The countries with the highest piracy rates are China, Japan, Korea, Germany, France, Brazil, Italy, Canada, and the United Kingdom. But piracy is also a problem in other countries. By some estimates, more than 90 percent of all business software used in Bulgaria, Indonesia, Russia, and Vietnam is pirated.

As a justification of high piracy rates, some observers point out that people in many countries simply might not be able to afford software that is priced for the U.S. market. This argument would make sense in China, where the average annual income is equivalent to about $3,500, and in North Korea, where the average income is only $900. A Korean who legitimately purchases Microsoft Office for $250 would be spending more than one-quarter of his or her annual income. Most of the countries with a high incidence of software piracy, however, have strong economies and respectable per capita incomes. To further discredit the theory that piracy stems from poverty, India—which has a fairly large computer-user community but a per capita income of only $1,600—is not among the top 10 countries with high rates of software piracy.

If economic factors do not account for the pervasiveness of software piracy, what does? Some analysts suggest that people need more education about software copyrights and the economic implications of piracy. Other analysts believe that copyright enforcement must be increased by supporting and implementing more vigorous efforts to identify and prosecute pirates.

▼ EXPAND THE IDEAS

1. Do you believe that software piracy is a serious issue? Write a two-page paper supporting your position. Include the opposing side's arguments in your report. Be sure to include your resources.

2. Do you think there are ways that software publishers can control piracy in the United States? In other countries? Do you know of any recent attempts at doing so? Work in a small group to brainstorm ideas and research recent trends or events. Compile your ideas and findings into a short presentation to give to the class. Include handouts for the audience and cite any sources you used.

3. Do you think that most software pirates understand that they are doing something illegal? Design a marketing campaign that could be used to educate the public about the issue. Create a poster that could be used in the campaign.

4. Should software publishers try to adjust software pricing for local markets? How would you propose such a pricing structure? How would these policies be enforced? Can you think of any other industry that adjusts prices for local markets? Write a two-page paper discussing your proposals and explaining your findings. Be sure to cite your sources.

End of Unit Exercises

▼ KEY TERMS

Absolute reference
Application software
Automatic recalculation
Cell
Cell reference
Clip art
Commercial software
Compiler
Computer language
Computer program
Computer programmer
Copyright
Copyright notice
Data management software
Data module
Database
Desktop operating system
Distribution disk
DOS
Field
File management software

File structure
Flat file
Formula
Frames
Freeware
Function
Graphical user interface (GUI)
Graphics
Graphics software
High-level languages
Horizontal market software
Install
Installation agreement
Interpreter
Label
Linux
Mac OS
Machine language
Main executable file
Microsoft Windows

MP3
MP3 player
Multitasking operating system
Multiuser operating system
Natural language query
Network operating system
Object code
Object-oriented database
Open source software
Operating system
Page layout
Public domain software
Query
Query by example
Query language
Record
Relational database
Relative reference
Scripts
Setup program

Shareware
Shrink-wrap license
Single-user operating system
Software
Software license
Source code
Spreadsheet
Spreadsheet software
SQL
Structured file
Support module
System requirements
System software
Table
Uninstall routine
UNIX
Utilities
Value
Vertical market software
Worksheet

▼ UNIT REVIEW

1. Use your own words to define each of the bold terms that appear throughout the unit. List 10 of the terms that are least familiar to you and write a sentence for each of them.

2. Make sure that you can list and describe the three types of files that are typically supplied on a software distribution disk.

3. Explain the difference between a compiler and an interpreter.

4. List three types of system software and at least five categories of application software.

5. Describe how an operating system manages resources.

6. Sketch a simple worksheet like one you might find in a spreadsheet software program and label the following: columns, rows, cell, active cell, values, labels, formulas, and Formula bar.

7. List three types of "number crunching" software that you can use instead of spreadsheet software and tell how you might use each one.

8. Describe when you would use each type of graphics software described in this unit.

9. Create a table with these column headings: single-user, multiuser, network, multitasking, and desktop operating system. List Linux, UNIX, Mac OS, and each version of Windows down the side of the table. Use a check mark to indicate which characteristics fit each operating system.

10. In your own words, explain what each of the ESRB ratings mean and how they would help you purchase software.

▼ FILL IN THE BEST ANSWER

1. Software can be divided into two major categories: application software and _____ software.

2. Software usually contains support modules and data modules, in addition to a main _____ file that you run to start the software.

3. Instructions that are written in a _____ -level language must be translated into _____ language before a computer can use them.

4. A(n) _____ translates all of the instructions in a program as a single batch, and the resulting machine language instructions are placed in a new file.

5. To run more than one program at a time, the operating system must allocate specific areas of _____ for each program.

6. A(n) _____ user interface provides a way for a user to interact with the software using a mouse and graphical objects on the screen.

7. A(n) _____ operating system is designed to deal with input, output, and processing requests from many users.

8. A(n) _____ operating system provides communications and routing services that allow computers to share data, programs, and peripheral devices.

9. Windows 2000 and Linux are classified as _____ operating systems, whereas Windows ME and Mac OS are classified as _____ operating systems.

10. Various kinds of document _____ software provide tools for creating and formatting printed and Web-based documents.

11. _____ management software is useful for working with flat files, whereas _____ management software works well with multiple files.

12. _____ software helps you work with wireframes, CAD drawings, photos, and slide presentations.

13. In a spreadsheet the rows are identified with _____ and the columns are identified with _____.

14. _____ market software is designed to automate specialized tasks in a specific market or business.

15. _____ art is a collection of drawings and photos designed to be inserted into documents.

16. _____ is a music compression file that stores digitized music in such a way that quality is excellent but the file size is relatively small.

17. _____ laws provide software authors with the exclusive right to copy, distribute, sell, and modify that work, except under special circumstances.

18. _____ is copyrighted software that is marketed with a "try before you buy" policy.

19. Linux is an example of open _____ software.

20. Public _____ software is not copyrighted, making it available for use without restriction, except that you cannot apply for a copyright on it.

▼ INDEPENDENT CHALLENGE 1

The word processor is one of the most widely used types of application software. Chances are, if you are learning to use the computer, you are also learning how to create documents with some word processing program. Based on your experience with word processing and your reading about document production software in this unit, complete the following independent challenge by writing a short paper discussing the following.

1. Describe the features of the word processing software that you use most often.

2. Explain how a spelling checker works and why it is not a substitute for proofreading.

3. Describe the strengths of word processing software.

4. Describe the weaknesses of word processing software.

▼ INDEPENDENT CHALLENGE 2

Word processing software, in particular, provides several features that automate tasks and allow you to work more productively. For example, suppose that you want to send prospective employers a letter and your resume. Rather than composing and addressing each letter individually, your software can perform a mail merge that automatically creates personalized letters by combining the information in a mailing list with a form letter.

1. Research document productivity software to identify automated features.

2. Create a table listing automated features as column heads and types of productivity software as row labels.

3. Use your research to complete the chart, using Xs to identify automated features available in various document production software.

4. Summarize your findings by writing a few paragraphs to answer the question: Does document production software increase productivity?

▼ INDEPENDENT CHALLENGE 3

How you acquire software varies based on the software and your needs. If you have a home computer and own or have purchased software, complete the following independent challenge by writing a short paper discussing the issues raised below.

1. What software is installed on your computer? How did you acquire the software? What type of software does each package fall into based on the categories outlined in this unit?

2. Explain the differences between commercial software, shareware, open source software, freeware, and public domain software. Do you have any of these? If so, which ones? Why did you select one type over the other?

3. If possible, describe one experience installing software, describe the process of installing software from a distribution CD, and contrast it with the process of installing downloaded software.

4. Have you used software that has an ESRB rating? Based on your experience with the software, did you find that the rating was adequate and fair? Why or why not?

▼ INDEPENDENT CHALLENGE 4

When you use a software package, it is important to understand the legal restrictions on its use. For this independent challenge, make a photocopy of the license agreement for any software package. Read the License agreement, then answer these questions:

1. Is this a shrink-wrap license? Why or why not?

2. After you pay your computer dealer for the program covered by this license, who owns the program?

3. Can you legally have one copy of the program on your computer at work and another copy of the program on your computer at home if you use the software only in one place at a time?

4. Can you legally sell the software? Why or why not?

5. Under what conditions can you legally transfer possession of the program to someone else?

6. If you were the owner of a software store, could you legally rent the program to customers if you were sure they did not keep a copy after the rental period was over?

7. Can you legally install this software on one computer, but give more than one user access to it?

8. If you use this program for an important business decision and later find out that a mistake in the program caused you to lose $500,000, what legal recourse is provided by the license agreement?

▼ INDEPENDENT CHALLENGE 5

 There are so many software packages on the market today that it is often overwhelming to make a wise purchasing decision. The breadth of software available in each category is quite large, and no two packages claim all the same features. Do you base your decision to buy a new application package on word of mouth? Reviewer comments in professional magazines? Trying it out? To complete this independent challenge, you will research a type of software package that you intend to purchase.

1. Determine the type of package you want to select (graphics, DTP, word processing, Web development, e-mail, scheduling, or data management) and which operating system you plan to use.

2. Locate vendor ads either on the Internet or in local papers or trade magazines that sell software.

3. Read comparison reviews of the products. Create a chart detailing the features and prepare a competitive analysis of the three top candidates for your purchase.

4. Write a short summary of your findings, indicating which package you would buy and why.

▼ VISUAL WORKSHOP

Operating systems are not unique to the PC and mainframe markets. Apple Computer has been developing operating systems for its computers since the early days of the Apple II computer. While the PC market has its share of versions from MS DOS to Windows XP, Apple Computer has developed its share of operating systems. Apple Computer has been using open-source projects to allow developers to enhance and customize Apple software. MAC OS X v. 10.1 is based on Darwin, which is the core of the MAC OS X. The source code for Darwin is freely available through Apple's public source project. Figure C-31 shows the Web page for Apple's latest offering of Mac OS.

FIGURE C-31

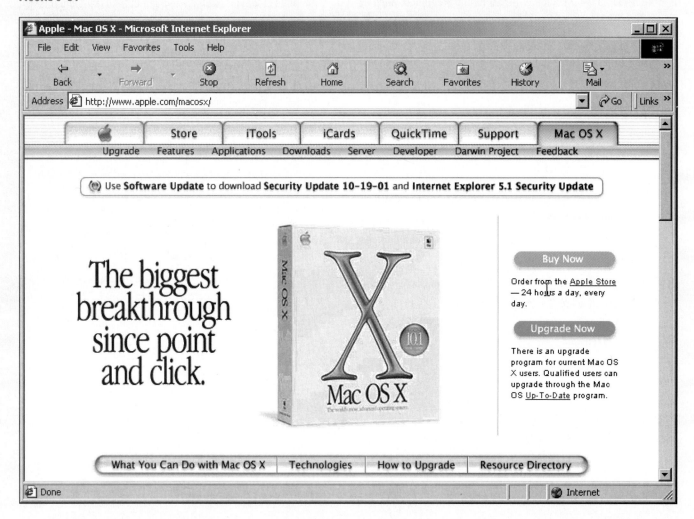

1. Log onto the Internet, then use your favorite search engine to research MAC OS. You might start by going to the Apple Computer Web site.

2. Research the various features that MAC OS supports. Write a brief list of the features and explain each one.

3. Research Darwin. List three new open-source projects that are currently in development.

4. Research the history of MAC OS. What new features does it have over the previous version?

UNIT D

Digital Electronics and File Management

OBJECTIVES

Introduce digital data representation
Introduce integrated circuits
Explore microprocessor performance factors
Understand computer memory: RAM
Explore computer memory
Introduce computer file basics
Understand file locations
Explore file management
Understand logical file storage
Use files
Understand physical file storage
Tech Talk: How a Microprocessor Executes Instructions

In this unit, you will learn how data representation and digital electronics work together to make computers tick. You will learn about two of the most important components in a computer—the microprocessor and memory. You will learn how they work and how they affect computer performance. You will learn about the different types of memory and how memory works to store and process data. You will get a general introduction to computer files and learn some very practical information about filenames. You will learn techniques for organizing computer files so that they are easy to access and update. You will also learn how an operating system stores, deletes, and tracks files. The Tech Talk section explains the details of how a microprocessor executes instructions.

Introducing digital data representation

Data representation refers to the form in which information is conceived, manipulated, and recorded. Because a computer is an electronic digital device, it uses electrical signals to represent data. A **digital device** works with discrete data or digits, such as 1 and 0, "on" and "off," or "yes" and "no." Data exists in the computer as a series of electronic signals represented as 1s and 0s, each of which is referred to as a **bit**. Most computer coding schemes use eight bits to represent each number, letter, or symbol. A series of eight bits is referred to as a **byte**. This lesson looks more closely at the coding schemes used in digital representation.

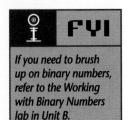

If you need to brush up on binary numbers, refer to the Working with Binary Numbers lab in Unit B.

DETAILS

- Just as Morse code uses dashes and dots to represent the letters of the alphabet, computers use sequences of bits to represent numbers, letters, punctuation marks, music, pictures, and videos. **Digital electronics** makes it possible for a computer to manipulate simple "on" and "off" signals to perform complex tasks. The **binary number system** allows computers to represent virtually any number simply by using 0s and 1s, which translate into electrical "on" and "off" signals.

- Digital computers use many different coding schemes to represent data. The coding scheme used by a computer depends on whether the data is numeric data or character data.

- **Numeric data** consists of numbers representing quantities that might be used in arithmetic operations. For example, your annual income is numeric data, as is your age. Computers represent numeric data using the binary number system, also called "base 2." The binary number system has only two digits: 0 and 1. These digits can be converted to electrical "ons" or "offs" inside a computer. The number 2 cannot be used in the binary number system; so instead of writing *2* you would write *10*, which you would pronounce as *one zero*. See Figure D-1.

- **Character data** is composed of letters, symbols, and numerals that will not be used in arithmetic operations. Examples of character data include your name, address, and hair color. Character data is also represented by a series of 1s and 0s.

- Several types of codes are used to represent character data, including ASCII, EBCDIC, and Unicode. **ASCII** (American Standard Code for Information Interchange) requires only seven bits for each character. For example, the ASCII code for an uppercase "A" is

1000001. ASCII provides codes for 128 characters, including uppercase letters, lowercase letters, punctuation symbols, and numerals. A superset of ASCII, called **Extended ASCII**, uses eight bits to represent each character. See Figure D-2. The eighth bit provides codes for 128 additional characters, which are usually boxes, circles, and other graphical symbols. **EBCDIC** (Extended Binary-Coded Decimal Interchange Code) is an alternative 8-bit code, usually used by older IBM mainframe computers. **Unicode** uses 16 bits and provides codes for 65,000 characters, a real bonus for representing the alphabets of multiple languages. Most personal computers use Extended ASCII code, although Unicode is becoming increasingly popular.

- Because computers represent numeric data with binary equivalents, ASCII codes that represent numbers might seem unnecessary. Computers, however, sometimes distinguish between numeric data and numerals. For example, you don't use your social security number in calculations, so a computer considers it character data composed of numerals, not numbers.

- To work with pictures and sounds, a computer must digitize the information that makes up the picture (such as the colors) and the information that makes up the sound (such as the notes) into 1s and 0s. Computers convert colors and notes into numbers, which can be represented by bits and stored in files as a long series of 1s and 0s.

- Your computer needs to know whether to interpret those 1s and 0s as ASCII code, binary numbers, or the code for a picture or sound. Most computer files contain a file header with information on the code that was used to represent the file data. A file header is stored along with the file and can be read by the computer, but never appears on the screen.

FIGURE D-1: Comparing decimal and binary numbers

▶ The decimal system uses ten symbols to represent numbers: 0, 1, 2, 3, 4, 5, 6, 7, 8, and 9; the binary number system uses only two symbols: 0 and 1

Decimal (Base 10)	Binary (Base 2)
0	0
1	1
2	10
3	11
4	100
5	101
6	110
7	111
8	1000
9	1001
10	1010
11	1011
1000	1111101000

FIGURE D-2: Extended ASCII code

▶ The extended ASCII code uses a series of eight 1s and 0s to represent 256 characters, including lowercase letters, upper-case letters, symbols, and numerals. The first 63 ASCII characters are not shown in this table because they represent special control sequences that cannot be printed.

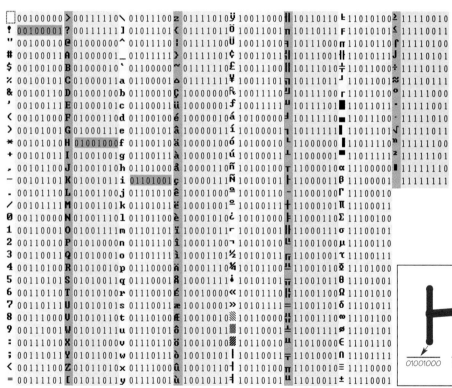

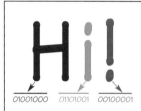

Quantifying bits and bytes

A bit is one binary digit and a byte is eight bits. Halfway between a "bit" and a "byte" is a nibble (four bits). The word "bit" can be abbreviated as a lowercase "b" and byte can be abbreviated as an uppercase "B."

Bits and bytes are used in different ways. Transmission speeds are usually expressed in bits, whereas storage space is usually expressed in bytes. The speed 56 Kbps means 56 kilobits per second; the capacity 8 GB means 8 gigabytes. "Kilo" is usually a prefix that means 1,000. For example, $50 K means $50,000. However, when it refers to bits or bytes, a "kilo" is 1,024 because computer engineers measure everything in base 2, and 2^{10} in base 2 is 1,024, not 1,000. So a **kilobit** (abbreviated Kb or Kbit) is 1,024 bits and a **kilobyte** (abbreviated KB or Kbyte) is 1,024 bytes. The prefix "mega" refers to a million, or in the context of bits and bytes, precisely 1,048,576 (the equivalent of 2^{20}). Mb or Mbit is the abbreviation for **megabit**. MB or Mbyte is the abbreviation for **megabyte**. The prefixes giga- (billion), tera- (trillion), and exa- (quintillion) can be used to quantify bits and bytes.

Introducing integrated circuits

Computers are electronic devices that use electrical signals and circuits to represent, process, and move data. Bits take the form of electrical pulses that can travel over circuits. An **integrated circuit (IC)** is a super-thin slice of semi-conducting material packed with microscopic circuit elements such as wires, transistors, capacitors, logic gates, and resistors. This lesson takes a closer look at integrated circuits and the important role they play in computers.

DETAILS

- If it weren't for the miniaturization made possible by digital electronics, computers would be huge, and the inside of a computer's system unit would contain a complex jumble of wires and other electronic components. Instead, today's computers contain relatively few parts. A computer's system unit contains circuit boards, storage devices, and a power supply that converts current from an AC wall outlet into the DC current used by computer circuitry. See Figure D-3.

- Integrated circuits can be used for microprocessors, memory, and support circuitry. The terms computer chip, microchip, and chip originated as jargon for integrated circuit.

- The microprocessor, memory modules, and support circuitry chips are packaged in a protective carrier or "chip package." Chip carriers vary in shape and size including small rectangular **DIPs (dual in-line packages)** with caterpillar-like legs protruding from a black, rectangular body; long, slim **DIMMs (dual in-line memory modules)**; pin-cushion-like **PGAs (pin-grid arrays)**; and cassette-like **SEC (single-edge contact cartridges) cartridges**, such as those pictured in Figure D-4. The pins on each chip package provides the electronic connection between the integrated circuit and other computer components.

- The computer's main circuit board, called a **motherboard** or main board, houses all essential chips and provides the connecting circuitry between them. See Figure D-5. If you look carefully at a motherboard, you'll see that some chips are permanently soldered in place. Other chips are plugged into special sockets and connectors, which allow chips to be removed for repairs or upgrades. When multiple chips are required for a single function, such as generating stereo-quality sound, the chips might be gathered together on a separate small circuit board, such as a sound card, which can be plugged into a special slot-like connector on the motherboard.

- A **microprocessor** (sometimes referred to as a processor) is an integrated circuit designed to process instructions. It is the most important component of a computer, and usually the most expensive single component. Looking inside a computer, you can usually identify the microprocessor because it is the largest chip on the motherboard. Depending on the brand and model, a microprocessor might be housed in a cartridge-like SEC cartridge or in a square PGA. Inside the chip carrier, a microprocessor is a very complex integrated circuit, containing as many as 50 million miniaturized electronic components. Some of these components are only 30 nanometers thick—a nanometer is 10^{-9} meter, or one-billionth of a meter. An atom is 10 nanometers thick.

Comparing today's microprocessors

A typical computer ad contains a long list of specifications describing a computer's components and capabilities. Most computer specifications begin with the microprocessor brand, type, and speed. Intel is the world's largest chipmaker and supplies a sizeable percentage of the microprocessors that power PCs. In 1971, Intel introduced the world's first microprocessor, the 4004. The company has continued to produce a steady stream of new processor models, beginning with the 8088 processor.

AMD (Advanced Micro Devices) is Intel's chief rival in the PC chip market. It produces microprocessors that work just like Intel's chips, but at a lower price. AMD's

Athlon processors are direct competitors to Intel's Pentium line and have a slight performance advantage according to some benchmarks. The Duron processor is AMD's "budget" model to compete with Intel's Celeron processors.

The microprocessors that are marketed with today's computers will handle most business, educational, and entertainment applications. While it is technically possible to upgrade your computer's microprocessor, the cost and technical factors discourage microprocessor upgrades.

FIGURE D-3: Inside a typical desktop computer

Power supply and fan —

Microprocessor with built-in fan —

Expansion cards —

— CD-ROM drive

— Floppy disk drive

— Hard disk drive

— Cables that transfer data from storage devices to motherboard

— Main circuit board (motherboard)

FIGURE D-4: Integrated circuits

▲ A DIP has two rows of pins that connect the IC circuitry to a circuit board

▲ A DIMM is a small circuit board containing several chips, typically used for memory

▲ A PGA is a square chip package with pins arranged in concentric squares, typically used for microprocessors

▲ An SEC cartridge is a popular chip package for microprocessors

FIGURE D-5: The motherboard

▶ A computer motherboard provides sockets for chips, slots for small circuit boards, and the circuitry that connects all these components

DIMM module containing memory chips

SEC-style microprocessor —

Connectors for storage device cables

Battery that powers the computer's real-time clock

Expansion slots hold additional expansion cards, such as a modem or sound card

Expansion card

DIP holding a ROM chip

Circuitry that transports data from one component to another

Connector for power supply

Exploring microprocessor performance factors

All microprocessors have two main parts: the **arithmetic logic unit (ALU)** and the **control unit**. To process data, each of these units performs specific tasks. The performance of a microprocessor is affected by several factors, including clock speed, word size, cache size, instruction set, and processing techniques. This lesson looks at the two main parts of a microprocessor and the factors that affect microprocessor performance.

DETAILS

- The ALU is the circuitry that performs arithmetic operations, such as addition and subtraction. It also performs logical operations, such as comparing two numbers using the logical operators such as less than (<), greater than (>), or equal to (=). Logical operations also allow for comparing characters and sorting and grouping information. The ALU uses **registers** to hold data that is being processed. Figure D-6 illustrates how the ALU works.

- The microprocessor's **control unit** fetches each instruction, as illustrated in Figure D-7. A microprocessor executes instructions that are provided by a computer program. The list of instructions that a microprocessor can perform is called its **instruction set**. These instructions are hard-wired into the processor's circuitry and include basic arithmetic and logical operations, fetching data, and clearing registers. A computer can perform very complex tasks, but it does so by performing a combination of simple tasks from its instruction set.

- How efficiently the ALU and the control unit work are determined by different performance factors. Processor speed is one of the most important indicators in determining the power of a computer system. The **microprocessor clock** is a timing device that sets the pace (the clock speed) for executing instructions. The clock speed of a microprocessor is specified in megahertz (MHz) or gigahertz (GHz) cycles per second. A cycle is the smallest unit of time in a microprocessor's universe. Every action that a processor performs is measured by these cycles. The clock speed is not equal to the number of instructions that a processor can execute in one second. In many computers, some instructions occur within one cycle, but other instructions might require multiple cycles. Some processors can even execute several instructions in a single clock cycle. A specification such as 1.3 GHz means that the microprocessor's clock operates at a speed of 1.3 billion cycles per second.

- **Word size**, another performance factor, refers to the number of bits that a microprocessor can manipulate at one time. Word size is based on the size of the registers in the ALU and the capacity of circuits that lead to those registers. A microprocessor with an 8-bit word size, for example, has 8-bit registers, processes eight bits at a time, and is referred to as an 8-bit processor. Processors with a larger word size can process more data during each processor cycle, a factor that leads to improved computer performance. Today's personal computers typically contain 32-bit or 64-bit processors.

- **Cache**, sometimes called RAM cache or cache memory, is special high-speed memory that a microprocessor can access more rapidly than memory elsewhere on the motherboard. Because it is another measure of performance, some computer ads specify cache type and capacity. Cache capacity is usually measured in kilobytes.

- Another performance factor is the type of instruction set a microprocessor uses. As chip designers developed various instruction sets for microprocessors, they tended to add increasingly more complex instructions, each of which required several clock cycles for execution. A microprocessor with such an instruction set uses **CISC (complex instruction set computer)** technology. A microprocessor with a limited set of simple instructions uses **RISC (reduced instruction set computer)** technology.

- The processing technique a microprocessor uses also affects performance. With **serial processing**, the processor must complete all of the steps in the instruction cycle before it begins to execute the next instruction. However, using a technology called **pipelining**, a processor can begin executing an instruction before it completes the previous instruction. Many of today's microprocessors also perform **parallel processing**, in which multiple instructions are executed at the same time.

FIGURE D-6: How the ALU works

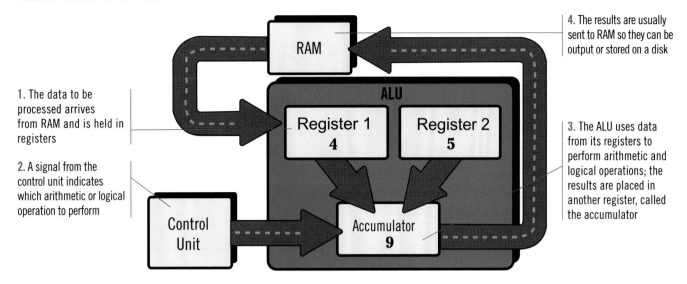

1. The data to be processed arrives from RAM and is held in registers

2. A signal from the control unit indicates which arithmetic or logical operation to perform

RAM

ALU

Register 1
4

Register 2
5

Control Unit

Accumulator
9

4. The results are usually sent to RAM so they can be output or stored on a disk

3. The ALU uses data from its registers to perform arithmetic and logical operations; the results are placed in another register, called the accumulator

FIGURE D-7: How the control unit works

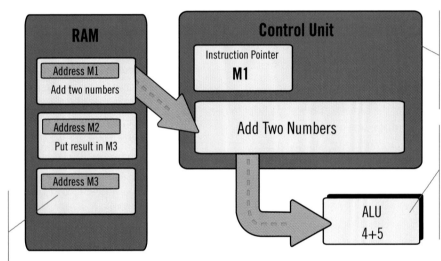

RAM

Address M1
Add two numbers

Address M2
Put result in M3

Address M3

Control Unit

Instruction Pointer
M1

Add Two Numbers

ALU
4+5

The control unit retrieves an instruction from RAM and puts it in the instruction register; the control unit interprets the instruction in its instruction register

Depending on the instruction, the control unit will get data from RAM, tell the ALU to perform an operation, or change the memory address of the instruction pointer

The RAM address of the instruction is kept in the instruction pointer; when the instruction has been executed, the address in the instruction pointer changes to indicate the RAM address of the next instruction to be executed

Benchmarking

All things being equal, a computer with a 1.3 GHz processor is faster than a computer with a 1 GHz processor and a computer with a processor that has a larger word size can process more data during each processor cycle than a computer with a processor that has a smaller word size. Furthermore, all things being equal, a computer with more Level 1 cache (L1), which is built into the processor chip, is faster than a computer with the same amount of Level 2 cache (L2), which is located on a separate chip and takes a little more time to get data to the processor.

But all things aren't equal. So how do you tell the overall performance of a computer and its microprocessor? Various testing laboratories run a series of tests called **benchmarks** to gauge the overall speed of a microprocessor. These results can be used to compare the results for other microprocessors. The results of benchmark tests are usually available on the Web and are published in computer magazine articles.

Understanding computer memory: RAM

Memory is the electronic circuitry linked directly to the processor that holds data and instructions when they are not being transported from one place to another. Computers use four categories of memory: random access memory (RAM), virtual memory, read-only memory (ROM), and CMOS memory. Each type of memory is characterized by the type of data it contains and the technology it uses to hold the data.

DETAILS

● **RAM** (random access memory) is a temporary holding area for data, application program instructions, and the operating system. In a personal computer, RAM is usually several chips or small circuit boards that plug into the motherboard within the computer's system unit. Next to the microprocessor, RAM is one of the most expensive computer components. The amount of RAM in a computer can, therefore, affect the overall price of a computer system. Along with processor speed, RAM capacity is the other most important factor in determining and comparing the power of a computer system.

● RAM is the "waiting room" for the computer's processor. Refer to Figure D-8. It holds raw data that is waiting to be processed and the program instructions for processing that data. In addition, RAM holds the results of processing until they can be stored more permanently on disk or tape.

● RAM also holds operating system instructions that control the basic functions of a computer system. These instructions are loaded into RAM every time you start your computer, and they remain there until you turn off your computer.

● People who are new to computers sometimes confuse RAM and disk storage, perhaps because both of these components hold data. To distinguish between RAM and disk storage, remember that RAM holds data in circuitry, whereas disk storage places data on storage media such as floppy disks, hard disks, or CDs. RAM is temporary storage; disk storage is more permanent. In addition, RAM usually has less storage capacity than disk storage.

● In RAM, microscopic electronic parts called **capacitors** hold the bits that represent data. You can visualize the capacitors as microscopic lights that can be turned on or off. Refer to Figure D-9. A charged capacitor is "turned on" and represents a "1" bit. A discharged capacitor is "turned off" and represents a "0" bit. You

can visualize the capacitors as being arranged in banks of eight. Each bank holds eight bits, or one byte, of data.

● Each RAM location has an address and holds one byte of data. A RAM address on each bank helps the computer locate data as needed for processing.

● In some respects, RAM is similar to a chalkboard. You can use a chalkboard to write mathematical formulas, erase them, and then write an outline for a report. In a similar way, RAM can hold numbers and formulas when you balance your checkbook, then hold the text of your English essay when you use word processing software. The contents of RAM can be changed just by changing the charge of the capacitors. Unlike a chalkboard, however, RAM is volatile, which means that it requires electrical power to hold data. If the computer is turned off, or if the power goes out, all data stored in RAM instantly and permanently disappears.

● The capacity of RAM is usually expressed in megabytes (MB). Today's personal computers typically feature between 64 and 512 MB of RAM. The amount of RAM needed by your computer depends on the software that you use. RAM requirements are routinely specified on the outside of a software package. If it turns out that you need more RAM, you can purchase and install additional memory up to the limit set by the computer manufacturer.

● RAM components vary in speed. RAM speed is often expressed in **nanoseconds**, or billionths of a second. Lower numbers mean faster transmission, processing, and storage of data. For example, 8 ns RAM is faster than 10 ns RAM. RAM speed can also be expressed in MHz (millions of cycles per second). Just the opposite of nanoseconds, higher MHz ratings mean faster speeds. For example, 100 MHz RAM is faster than 80 MHz RAM.

FIGURE D-8: Contents of RAM

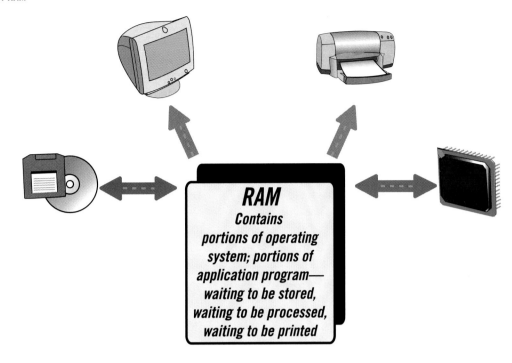

FIGURE D-9: How RAM works

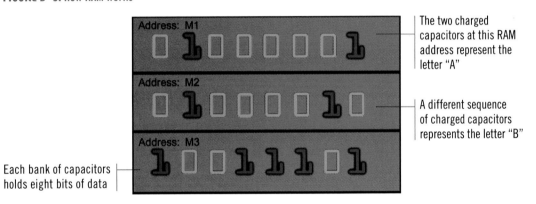

The two charged capacitors at this RAM address represent the letter "A"

A different sequence of charged capacitors represents the letter "B"

Each bank of capacitors holds eight bits of data

Different types of RAM

Most of today's personal computers use **SDRAM** (Figure D-10) or RDRAM. SDRAM (synchronous dynamic RAM) is fast and relatively inexpensive. **RDRAM** (Rambus dynamic RAM) was first developed for the popular Nintendo 64® game system, and was adapted for use in personal computers in 1999. Although more expensive than SDRAM, RDRAM is usually paired with microprocessors that run at speeds faster than 1 GHz because it can somewhat increase overall system performance. RAM is usually configured as a series of DIPs soldered onto a small circuit board called a **DIMM** (dual in-line memory module), **RIMM** (Rambus in-line memory module), or **SO-RIMM** (small outline Rambus in-line memory module). DIMMs contain SDRAM, whereas RIMMs and SO-RIMMs contain RDRAM.

FIGURE D-10

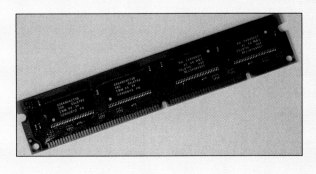

Exploring computer memory

In addition to RAM, a computer uses three other types of memory: virtual memory, ROM, and CMOS. This lesson looks at these types of computer memory and how all computer memory types work together.

DETAILS

● It might seem logical that the more you do with your computer, the more memory it needs. However, if you want to work with several programs and large graphics at the same time, personal computer operating systems are quite adept at allocating RAM space to multiple programs. If a program exceeds the allocated space, the operating system uses an area of the hard disk called **virtual memory** to store parts of a program or data file until they are needed. By selectively exchanging the data in RAM with the data in virtual memory, your computer effectively gains almost unlimited memory capacity.

One disadvantage of virtual memory is reduced performance. Too much dependence on virtual memory can have a negative affect on your computer's performance because getting data from a mechanical device, such as a hard disk, is much slower than getting data from an electronic device, such as RAM. Loading up your computer with as much RAM as possible will help your computer speed through all of its tasks.

● **ROM (read-only memory)** is a type of memory circuitry that holds the computer's startup routine. ROM is housed in a single integrated circuit, usually a fairly large, caterpillar-like DIP package that is plugged into the motherboard.

While RAM is temporary and volatile, ROM is permanent and non-volatile. ROM circuitry holds "hard-wired" instructions that remain in place even when the computer power is turned off. This is a familiar concept to anyone who has used a hand calculator, which includes various "hard-wired" routines for calculating square roots, cosines, and other functions. The instructions in ROM are permanent, and the only way to change them is to replace the ROM chip.

PROM (programmable read-only memory) is read-only memory that can be created by a user with a special machine through a process called "burning." ROM chips that can be erased and reused using another technique are **EPROM (erasable programmable read-only memory)**.

● When you turn on your computer, the microprocessor receives electrical power and is ready to begin executing instructions. But, because the power had been off, RAM is empty and contains no instructions for the microprocessor to execute. Now ROM plays its part. ROM contains a small set of instructions called the **ROM BIOS (basic input/output system)**. See Figure D-11. These instructions tell the computer how to access the hard disk, find

the operating system, and load it into RAM. Once the operating system is loaded, the computer can understand your input, display output, run software, and access your data. While ROM BIOS instructions are accomplished mainly without user intervention or knowledge, the computer will not function without the ROM chip and the BIOS instructions.

● In order to operate correctly, a computer must have some basic information about storage, memory, and display configurations. For example, your computer needs to know how much memory is available so that it can allocate space for all of the programs that you want to run. RAM goes blank when the computer power is turned off, so configuration information cannot be stored there. ROM would not be a good place for this information either because it holds data on a permanent basis. If, for example, your computer stored memory specification information in ROM, you could never add more memory; or if you were able to add it, you couldn't change the memory specification information in ROM. To store some basic system information, your computer needs a type of memory that's more permanent than RAM but less permanent than ROM.

● **CMOS memory (complementary metal oxide semiconductor)**, pronounced "SEE moss," is a type of memory that requires very little power to hold data. CMOS memory is stored on a chip that can be powered by a small, rechargeable battery integrated into the motherboard. The battery trickles power to the CMOS chip so that it can retain vital data about your computer system configuration even when your computer is turned off.

When you change the configuration of your computer system by adding RAM, for example, the data in CMOS must be updated. Some operating systems recognize such changes and automatically perform the update; or you can manually change CMOS settings by running the CMOS setup program. See Figure D-12.

● Even though virtual memory, ROM, and CMOS have important roles in the operation of a computer, it is really RAM capacity that makes a difference you can notice. The more data and programs that can fit into RAM, the less time your computer will spend moving data to and from virtual memory. With lots of RAM, you'll find that documents scroll faster, and many graphics operations take less time than with a computer that has less RAM capacity.

FIGURE D-11: ROM BIOS

ROM BIOS is housed in one or more ROM chips on the motherboard

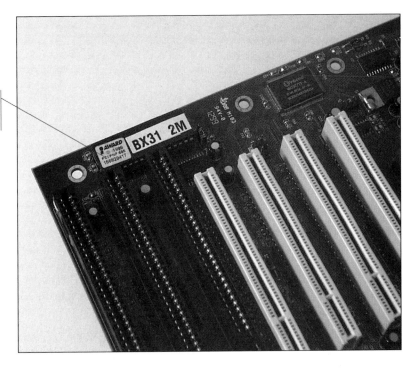

FIGURE D-12: CMOS setup program

▶ CMOS holds computer configuration settings, such as the date and time, hard disk capacity, number of floppy disk drives, and RAM capacity

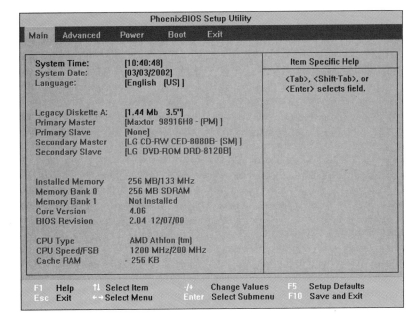

PhoenixBIOS Setup Utility

| Main | Advanced | Power | Boot | Exit |

System Time:	[10:40:48]
System Date:	[03/03/2002]
Language:	[English [US]]

Item Specific Help

<Tab>, <Shift-Tab>, or <Enter> selects field.

Legacy Diskette A:	[1.44 Mb 3.5"]
Primary Master	[Maxtor 98916H8 - (PM)]
Primary Slave	[None]
Secondary Master	[LG CD-RW CED-8080B- [SM]]
Secondary Slave	[LG DVD-ROM DRD-8120B]

Installed Memory	256 MB/133 MHz
Memory Bank 0	256 MB SDRAM
Memory Bank 1	Not Installed
Core Version	4.06
BIOS Revision	2.04 12/07/00

CPU Type	AMD Athlon (tm)
CPU Speed/FSB	1200 MHz/200 MHz
Cache RAM	256 KB

| F1 | Help | ↑↓ Select Item | -/+ | Change Values | F5 | Setup Defaults |
| Esc | Exit | ←→ Select Menu | Enter | Select Submenu | F10 | Save and Exit |

FYI

The difference between memory types: RAM is temporary; virtual memory is disk-based; ROM is permanent; CMOS is battery-powered and more permanent than RAM but less permanent than ROM.

Introducing computer file basics

The term "file" was used for filing cabinets and collections of papers long before it became part of the personal computer lexicon. Today, a **computer file** or simply "file" is defined as a named collection of data that exists on a storage medium, such as a hard disk, floppy disk, CD, DVD, or tape. A file can contain a group of records, a document, a photo, music, a video, an e-mail message, or a computer program. This lesson looks at several common characteristics of computer files—type, filename, and format.

DETAILS

- There are several categories of files, such as data files, executable files, configuration files, drivers, and modules. A computer file is classified according to the data it contains, the software that was used to create it, and the way you should use it. See Table D-1.

- Every file has a filename. The filename has two parts—the filename itself and the filename extension.

- A **filename** is a unique set of characters and numbers that identifies a file and should describe its contents. When you save a file, you must provide it with a valid filename that adheres to specific rules, referred to as **file-naming conventions**. Each operating system has a unique set of file-naming conventions. See Figure D-13.

  If an operating system attaches special significance to a symbol, you might not be able to use it in a filename. For example, Windows uses the colon (:) and the backslash (\) to separate the device letter from a filename or folder, as in C:\Music. A filename such as Report:\2002 is not valid because the operating system would become confused about how to interpret the colon and backslash.

  Some operating systems also contain a list of **reserved words** that are used as commands or special identifiers. You cannot use these words alone as a filename. You can, however, use these words as part of a longer filename. For example, under Windows XP, the filename Nul would not be valid, but you could name a file something like Nul Committee Notes.doc.

- A **filename extension** (or file extension) is separated from the main filename by a period, as in Paint.exe. A filename extension further describes the file contents. Generally, the software application you are using automatically assigns the filename extension when you save a file. If you don't see a file-

name extension when you use the Save or Save as dialog box to save a file, the option to show filename extensions has been deactivated. When using Windows, you can choose to hide (but not erase) or display the filename extensions through the Folder Options setting in the Control Panel.

  Knowledge of filename extensions comes in handy when you receive a file on a disk or over the Internet but you don't know much about its contents. If you are familiar with filename extensions, you will know the file format and, therefore, which application to use when you want to open the file.

- A filename extension is usually related to the **file format**, which is defined as the arrangement of data in a file and the coding scheme that is used to represent the data. Files that contain graphics are usually stored using a different file format than files containing text. Hundreds of file formats exist, and you'll encounter many of them as you use a variety of software. As you work with a variety of files, you will begin to recognize that some filename extensions, such as .txt (text file) or .jpg (graphics file), indicate a file type and are not specific to application software.

  You will also recognize that other filename extensions, such as .doc (Word), .xls (Excel), and .zip (Winzip), can help you identify which application was used to create the file. These filename extensions indicate the **native file format**, which is the file format used to store files created with that software program. For example, Microsoft Word stores files in doc format, whereas Adobe Illustrator stores graphics files in ai format. When using a software application such as Microsoft Word to open a file, the program displays any files that have the filename extension for its native file format, as shown in Figure D-14.

FIGURE D-13: File-naming conventions

	DOS AND WINDOWS 3.1	WINDOWS 95/98/ME/XP/ NT/2000	MAC OS	UNIX/LINUX
Maximum length of filename	8-character filename plus an extension of 3 characters or less	255-character filename including an extension of up to 3 characters	31 characters (no extensions)	14–256 characters (depending on UNIX/Linux version) including an extension of any length
Spaces allowed	No	Yes	Yes	No
Numbers allowed	Yes	Yes	Yes	Yes
Characters not allowed	* / [ ] ; " = \ : ,	?	* \ : < >	" / ?	None	* ! @ # $ % ^ & ( ) { } [ ] " \ ? ; < >
Filenames not allowed	Aux, Com1, Com2, Com3, Com4, Con, Lpt1, Lpt2, Lpt3, Prn, Nul	Aux, Com1, Com2, Com3, Com4, Con, Lpt1, Lpt2, Lpt3, Prn, Nul	None	Depends on the version of UNIX or Linux
Case sensitive	No	No	Yes	Yes (use lowercase)

FIGURE D-14: Filename extensions

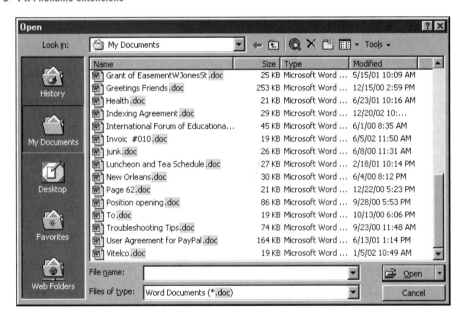

TABLE D-1: Types of files

TYPE OF FILE	DESCRIPTION	EXTENSION
Batch file	A sequence of operating system commands that is executed automatically when the computer boots	.bat
Configuration file	Information about programs that the computer uses to allocate the resources necessary to run them	.cfg .sys .mif .bin .ini
Help	The information that is displayed by online Help	.hlp
Temporary file	Contains data while a file is open, but that is discarded when you close the file	.tmp
Program modules	The main executable files for a computer program	.exe .com
Support modules	Program instructions that are executed in conjunction with the main .exe file for a program	.ocx .vbx .vbs .dll

Understanding file locations

Programs and data files have unique names and locations to ensure that the computer can find them. To designate a file's location, you must specify where the file is stored on the storage media. This lesson looks more closely at file locations—how to assign them and the information about each file that is available at the file's location.

DETAILS

• Each storage device on a PC is identified by a device letter. The floppy disk drive is usually assigned device letter A and is referred to as "drive A." A device letter is usually followed by a colon, so drive A could be designated as A: or as 3½" Floppy (A:). The main hard disk drive is usually referred to as "drive C." Additional storage devices can be assigned letters from D through Z. Although most PCs stick to the standard of drive A for the floppy disk drive and drive C for the hard disk drive, the device letters for CD, Zip, and DVD drives are not standardized. For example, the CD-writer on your computer might be assigned device letter E, whereas the CD-writer on another computer might be assigned device letter R.

• An operating system maintains a list of files called a **directory** for each storage disk, tape, CD, or DVD. The main directory of a disk is referred to as the **root directory**. On a PC, the root directory is typically identified by the device letter followed by a backslash. For example, the root directory of the hard disk drive would be C:\. You should try to avoid storing your data files in the root directory of your hard disk, and instead store them in a subdirectory.

• A root directory is often subdivided into smaller lists called **subdirectories**. When you use Windows, Mac OS, or a Linux graphical file manager, these subdirectories are depicted as **folders** because they work like the folders in a filing cabinet to store an assortment of related items. Each folder has a name, so you can easily create a folder called Documents to hold reports, letters, and so on. You can create another folder called Music to hold your MP3 files. Folders can be created within other folders. You might, for example, create a folder within your Music folder to hold your jazz collection and another to hold your reggae collection.

A folder name is separated from a drive letter and other folder names by a special symbol.

In Microsoft Windows, this symbol is the backslash (\). For example, the folder for your reggae music (within the Music folder on drive C) would be written as C:\Music\Reggae.

Imagine how hard it would be to find a specific piece of paper in a filing cabinet that was stuffed with a random assortment of reports, letters, and newspaper clippings. By storing a file in a folder, you assign it a place in an organized hierarchy of folders and files.

• A computer file's location is defined by a **file specification** (sometimes called a **path**), which begins with the drive letter and is followed by the folder(s), filename, and filename extension. Suppose that you have stored an MP3 file called Marley One Love in the Reggae folder on your hard disk drive. Its file specification would be as shown in Figure D-15.

• A file contains data, stored as a group of bits. The more bits, the larger the file. **File size** is usually measured in bytes, kilobytes, or megabytes. Knowing the size of a file can be important especially when you are sending a file as an e-mail attachment. Your computer's operating system keeps track of file sizes.

• Your computer keeps track of the date on which a file was created or last modified. The **file date** is useful if you have created several versions of a file and want to make sure that you know which version is the most recent. It can also come in handy if you have downloaded several updates of player software, such as an MP3 player, and you want to make sure that you install the latest version.

• The operating system keeps track of file locations, filenames, filename extensions, file size, and file dates. See Figure D-16. This information is always available to you through a file management utility, which will be discussed in the next lesson.

FIGURE D-15: A file specification

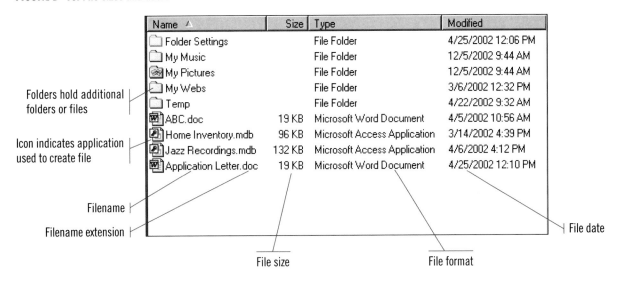

C:\Music\Reggae\Marley One Love.mp3

| Drive letter | Primary folder | Secondary folder | Filename | Filename extension |

FIGURE D-16: File sizes and dates

Name △	Size	Type	Modified
Folder Settings		File Folder	4/25/2002 12:06 PM
My Music		File Folder	12/5/2002 9:44 AM
My Pictures		File Folder	12/5/2002 9:44 AM
My Webs		File Folder	3/6/2002 12:32 PM
Temp		File Folder	4/22/2002 9:32 AM
ABC.doc	19 KB	Microsoft Word Document	4/5/2002 10:56 AM
Home Inventory.mdb	96 KB	Microsoft Access Application	3/14/2002 4:39 PM
Jazz Recordings.mdb	132 KB	Microsoft Access Application	4/6/2002 4:12 PM
Application Letter.doc	19 KB	Microsoft Word Document	4/25/2002 12:10 PM

Folders hold additional folders or files

Icon indicates application used to create file

Filename

Filename extension

File size

File format

File date

Deleting files

You may have noticed when using Windows that when you delete a file it is moved to the Recycle Bin. The Windows Recycle Bin and similar utilities in other operating systems are designed to protect you from accidentally deleting hard disk files that you actually need. The operating system moves the file to the Recycle Bin folder. The "deleted" file still takes up space on the disk, but does not appear in the usual directory listing. The file does, however, appear in the directory listing for the Recycle Bin folder, and you can undelete any files in this listing.

To delete data from a disk in such a way that no one can ever read it, you can use special file shredder software that overwrites "empty" sectors with random 1s and 0s. You might find this software handy if you plan to donate your computer to an organization, and you want to make sure that your personal data no longer remains on the hard disk. It is important to remember that only files you delete from your hard disk drive are sent to the Recycle Bin; files you delete from a floppy disk drive are not sent to the Recycle Bin.

Exploring file management

File management encompasses any procedure that helps you organize your computer-based files so that you can find and use them more efficiently. Depending on your computer's operating system, you may be able to organize and manipulate your files from within an application program, or by using a special file management utility provided by the operating system.

DETAILS

- Applications, such as word processing software or graphics software, typically provide file management capabilities for files created within the application. For example, most applications provide a way to open files and save them in a specific folder on a designated storage device. An application might also provide additional file management capabilities, such as deleting and renaming files.

- Most application software provides access to file management tasks through the Save and Open dialog boxes. The Save As dialog box that is displayed by Windows applications allows you to do more than just save a file. You can use it to perform other file management tasks such as rename a file, delete a file, or create a folder, as shown in Figure D-18. At times, however, you might want to work with groups of files, or perform other file operations that are inconvenient within the Save or Open dialog boxes. Most operating systems

provide **file management utilities** that give you the "big picture" of the files you have stored on your disks and help you work with them. For example, Windows provides **Windows Explorer**, which is a file management utility that is bundled with the Windows operating system. On computers with Mac OS, the file management utility is called Finder. These utilities, shown in Figure D-19, help you view a list of files, find files, move files from one place to another, make copies of files, delete files, and rename files.

- File management utilities are designed to help you organize and manipulate the files that are stored on your computer. Most file management operations begin with locating a particular file or folder. A file management utility should make it easy to find what you're looking for by drilling down through your computer's hierarchy of folders and files.

The Save v. Save As dialog box

Knowing how to save a file is a crucial file management skill. The Save As command is generally an option on the File menu. In addition to the Save As option, the menu also contains a Save option. The difference between the two options is subtle, but useful. The Save As option allows you to select a name and storage device for a file, whereas the Save option simply saves the latest version of a file under its current name and at its current location. When you try to use the Save option for a file that doesn't yet have a name, your application will display the Save As dialog box, even though you selected the Save option. The flow chart in Figure D-17 will help you decide whether to use the Save or Save As command.

FIGURE D-17: Save or Save As

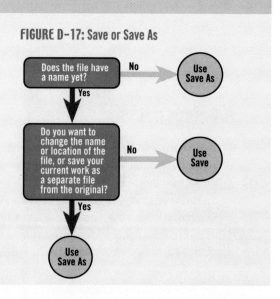

FIGURE D-18: The Save As dialog box

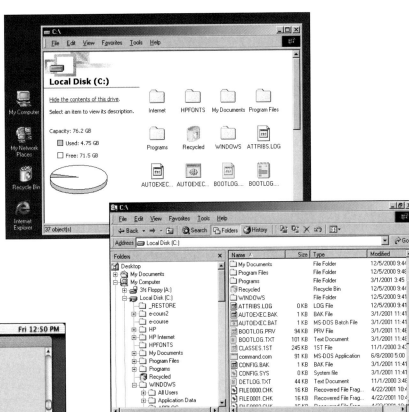

Click this button to create a new folder

To rename or delete a folder, right-click it and then use one of the options on the shortcut menu

To rename or delete a file, right-click the filename, then select a command from the shortcut menu that appears; in addition to the Rename and Delete options, this menu might also include options to print the file, e-mail it, or scan it for viruses

FIGURE D-19: Operating system file managers

▶ The Windows File Manager utility can be tailored to show files as icons or as a list

▼ Mac OS provides a file management utility called the Finder

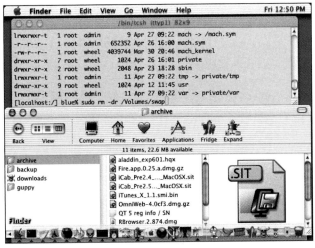

Understanding logical file storage

File management utilities often use some sort of metaphor to help you visualize and mentally organize the files on your disks and other storage devices. These metaphors are sometimes referred to as **logical storage models** because they help you form a mental (logical) picture of the way in which your files are stored. Windows Explorer is based on logical file storage. This lesson looks at a logical file storage metaphor and how Windows Explorer implements that model.

DETAILS

● After hearing so much about files and folders, you might have guessed that the filing cabinet is a popular metaphor for computer storage. In this metaphor, each storage device of a computer corresponds to one of the drawers in a filing cabinet. The drawers hold folders and the folders hold files, as illustrated in Figure D-20.

You might also find it helpful to think of the logical storage model as an outline. In the hierarchy of an outline, the highest or top level is the general level (root directory). As you move down to lower levels in the outline you have greater detail (primary subfolders and then secondary subfolders and so on). When you expand a higher level (a folder), you can see all the subordinate (subfolder) levels for that folder.

● Figure D-21 shows how Microsoft programmers used the filing cabinet metaphor within the file management utility called Windows Explorer.

The Windows Explorer window is divided into two "window panes." The pane on the left side of the window lists each of the storage devices connected to your computer, plus several important system objects, such as My Computer, Network Neighborhood, and the Desktop. Each storage device is synonymous with a file drawer in the file cabinet metaphor.

An icon for a storage device or other system object can be "expanded" by clicking its corresponding plus-sign icon. Once an icon is opened, its contents appear in the pane on the right side of the Windows Explorer window. Opening an icon displays the next level of the storage hierarchy, usually a collection of folders. Each folder is synonymous with the folders in the file cabinet metaphor.

Any of these folders can contain files or subfolders. Files are synonymous with papers in the file cabinet metaphor. Subfolders can be further expanded by clicking their plus-sign icons. You continue expanding folders in this manner until you reach the file you need.

The minus-sign icon can be used to collapse a device or folder to hide the levels of the hierarchy.

● To work with either a single or a group of files or folders, you must first select them. Windows Explorer displays all of the items that you select by highlighting them. Once a folder or file or a group of folders or files are highlighted, you can use the same copy, move, or delete procedure that you would use for a single item.

● In addition to locating files and folders, Windows Explorer provides a set of file management tools that will help you manipulate files and folders in the following ways:

* Rename. You might want to change the name of a file or folder to better describe its contents. When renaming a file, you should be careful to keep the same filename extension so that you can open it with the correct application software.

* Copy. You can copy a file or folder. For example, you can copy a file from your hard disk to a floppy disk if you want to send it to a friend or colleague. You might also want to make a copy of a document so that you can revise the copy and leave the original intact. When you copy a file, the file remains in the original location and a duplicate file is added to a different location—two copies of the same file now exist but with different paths.

* Move. You can move a file from one folder to another, or from one storage device to another. When you move a file, it is erased from its original location, so make sure that you remember the new location of the file. You can also move folders from one storage device to another, or from one folder to another.

* Delete. You can delete a file when you no longer need it. You can also delete a folder. Be careful when you delete a folder because most file management utilities also delete all the files (and subfolders) that a folder contains.

FIGURE D-20: A filing cabinet as a metaphor

The file cabinet represents all of the storage devices connected to a computer

Each drawer represents one storage device

A drawer can contain folders that hold documents and other folders

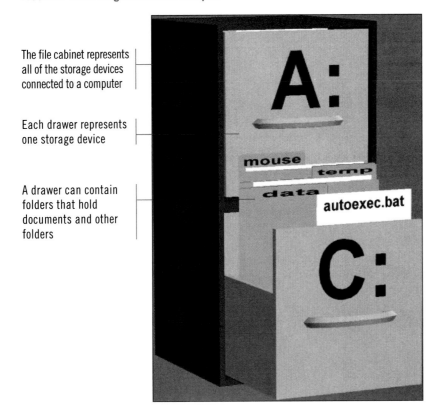

FIGURE D-21: Windows Explorer

► Windows Explorer borrows the folders from the filing cabinet metaphor and places them in a hierarchical structure, which makes it easy to drill down through the levels of the directory hierarchy to locate a folder or file

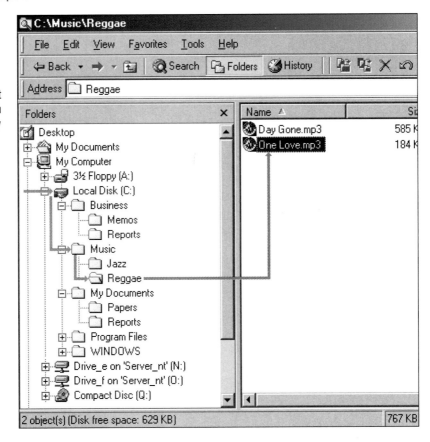

Using files

As you will recall, most users create, open, or save data files using application software. You are now ready to apply what you've learned about files and file management to see how you would typically use files when you work with application software. Using word processing software to produce a document is a common way to use files on a computer, so we'll take a look at the file operations for a typical word processing session. Examine Figure D-22 to get an overview of the file activities of a typical word processing session.

FIGURE D-22

1. Running an Application

Suppose you want to create a document about the summer vacation packages your company offers. You decide to create the document using the word processing software, Microsoft Word. Your first step is to start the Word program. When you run Word, the program file is copied from the hard drive to the memory of the computer.

2. Creating a File

You begin to type the text of the document. As you type, your data is stored in the memory of the computer. Your data will not be stored on disk until you initiate the Save command.

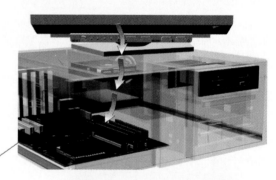

Word.exe is loaded into memory from the hard disk

Your data is stored in memory while you type

A:Vacation.doc is copied from memory to the floppy disk

3. Saving a Data File

When you create a file and save it on disk for the first time, you must name the file so that you can later retrieve it by name. Earlier in this unit, you learned that the name you give to a file must follow the file-naming conventions for the operating system. You name the file *A:Vacation.doc*. By typing *A:* you direct the computer to save the file on the floppy disk in drive A. The computer looks for empty clusters on the disk where it can store the file. It then adds the filename to the directory, along with the number of the cluster that contains the beginning of the file. Once you have saved your file, you can continue to work on the document, exit the Word program, or work on another document.

Word.exe is loaded into memory

A:Vacation.doc is copied from disk into memory

4. Retrieving a Data File

Suppose that a few days later, you decide that you want to re-read *Vacation.doc*. You need to start Microsoft Word. Once the Word program is running, you can retrieve the *Vacation.doc* file from the disk on which it is stored.

When you want to use a data file that already exists on disk storage, you must tell the application to open the file. In Microsoft Word, you either type the name of the file, *A:Vacation.doc*, or select the filename from a list of files stored on the disk. The application communicates the filename to the operating system.

The operating system looks at the directory and FAT to find which clusters contain the file, then moves the read-write head to the appropriate disk location to read the file. The electronics on the disk drive transfer the file data into the main memory of the computer, where your application software can manipulate it. Once the operating system has retrieved the file, the word processing software displays it on the screen.

The changes you make to the document are stored in memory; when you save your revisions, they overwrite the previous version of *Vacation.doc*

5. Revising a Data File

When you see the *Vacation.doc* file on the screen, you can modify it. Each character that you type and each change that you make are stored temporarily in the main memory of the computer, but not on the disk.

The *Vacation.doc* file is already on the disk, so when you are done with the modifications you have two options. Option 1 is to store the revised version in place of the old version. Option 2 is to create a new file for your revision and give it a different name, such as *Holiday.doc*.

If you decide to go with option 1—store the revised version in place of the old version—the operating system copies your revised data from the computer memory to the same clusters that contained the old file. You do not have to take a separate step to delete the old file—the operating system automatically records the new file over it.

If you decide to go with option 2—create a new file for the revision—the application prompts you for a filename. Your revisions will be stored under the new filename. The original file, *Vacation.doc*, will remain on the disk in its unrevised form.

Understanding physical file storage

So far, you've seen how an operating system like Windows can help you visualize computer storage as files and folders. The structure of files and folders that you see in Windows Explorer is called a "logical" model, because it helps you create a mental picture. You have also seen how files are created, saved, retrieved, and revised during a typical word processing session. What actually happens to a file when you save it is called physical file storage.

DETAILS

- Before a computer can store data, the storage medium must be formatted so that it contains the equivalent of electronic storage bins. This is accomplished by dividing a disk into **tracks**, and dividing each track into wedge-shaped **sectors**, both of which are created when a disk or disk drive is formatted. See Figure D-23. Tracks and sectors are numbered to provide addresses for each data storage bin. The numbering scheme depends on the storage device and the operating system. On CDs and DVDs, one or more tracks spiral out from the center of the disk; on floppy, Zip, and hard disks, tracks are arranged as concentric circles.

  Today, most floppy, Zip, and hard disks are preformatted at the factory to meet the specifications of a particular operating system; however, computer operating systems provide formatting utilities that you can use to reformat some storage devices such as floppy and hard disks. The companies that manufacture hard disk drives, writable CD drives, and writable DVD drives also supply formatting utilities. Windows includes a floppy disk formatting utility. When you use a formatting utility, it erases any data that happens to be on the disk, then prepares the tracks and sectors necessary to hold data.

- The operating system uses a **file system** to keep track of the names and locations of files that reside on a storage medium, such as a hard disk. Different operating systems use different file systems. Most versions of Mac OS use the Macintosh Hierarchical File System (HFS). Ext2fs (extended 2 file system) is the native file system for Linux. Windows NT, Windows 2000, and Windows XP use a file system called New Technology FileSystem (NTFS). Windows versions 95, 98, and ME use a file system called FAT32.

- To speed up the process of storing and retrieving data, a disk drive usually works with a group of sectors called a **cluster** or a "block." The number of sectors that form a cluster varies depending on the capacity of the disk and how the operating system works with files. A file system's primary task is to maintain a list of clusters and keep track of which ones are empty and which ones hold data. This information is stored in a special file.

- If your computer uses the FAT32 file system, for example, this special file is called the **File Allocation Table** (FAT). Each of your disks contains its own FAT, so that information about its contents is always available when the disk is in use. Unfortunately, storing this crucial file on disk presents a risk; if the FAT is damaged by a hard disk head crash, a computer virus, or scratch, you'll generally lose access to all of the data that is stored on the disk.

- When you save a file, your PC's operating system looks at the FAT to see which clusters are empty. It will select one of these clusters, record the file data there, and then revise the FAT to include the filename and its location. A file that does not fit into a single cluster spills over into the next contiguous (meaning adjacent) cluster unless that cluster already contains data. When contiguous clusters are not available, the operating system stores parts of a file in noncontiguous (nonadjacent) clusters. Figure D-24 helps you visualize how the FAT keeps track of filenames and locations.

- When you want to retrieve a file, the OS looks through the FAT for the filename and its location. It directs the disk drive's read-write head to move to the first cluster that contains the file data. Using additional data from the FAT, the operating system can move the read-write head to each of the clusters that contain the remaining parts of the file.

- When you click a file's icon and then select the delete option, the operating system simply changes the status of the file's clusters to "empty" and removes the filename from the FAT. The filename no longer appears in a directory listing, but the file's data remains in the clusters until a new file is stored there. You might think that this data is erased, but it is possible to purchase utilities that recover a lot of this "deleted" data. Law enforcement agents, for example, use these utilities to gather evidence from "deleted" files on the computer disks of suspected criminals.

- As a computer writes files on a disk, parts of files tend to become scattered all over the disk. These **fragmented files** are stored in noncontiguous clusters. Drive performance generally declines as the read-write heads move back and forth to locate the clusters that contain the parts of a file. To regain peak performance, you can use a **defragmentation utility** to rearrange the files on a disk so that they are stored in contiguous clusters. See Figure D-25.

FIGURE D-23: Formatting a disk

▶ Formatting prepares the surface of a disk to hold data
▶ Disks are divided into tracks and wedge-shaped sectors—each side of a floppy disk typically has 80 tracks divided into 18 sectors; each sector holds 512 bytes of data
▶ On a typical CD, a single track is about three miles long and is divided into 336,000 sectors; each sector holds 2,048 bytes of data

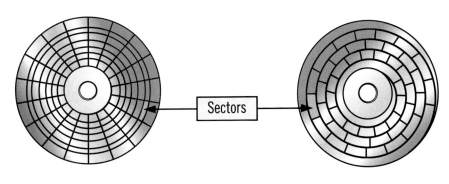

Sectors

FIGURE D-24: How the FAT works

▶ Each colored cluster on the disk contains part of a file; clusters 3 and 4 (blue) contain the *Bio.txt* file
▶ Cluster 9 (aqua) contains the *Pick.wps* file; clusters 7, 8, and 10 contain the *Jordan.wks* file
▶ A computer locates and displays the *Jordan.wks* file, by looking for its name in the File Allocation Table; by following the pointers listed in the Status column, the computer can then see that the file is continued in clusters 8 and 10

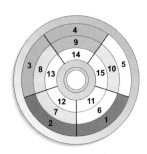

File Allocation Table

CLUSTER	STATUS	COMMENT
1	1	Reserved for operating system
2	1	Reserved for operating system
3	4	First cluster of Bio.txt. Points to cluster 4, which holds more data for Bio.txt
4	999	Last cluster for Bio.txt
5	0	Empty
6	0	Empty
7	8	First cluster for Jordan.wks. Points to cluster 8, which holds more data for the Jordan.wks file
8	10	Second cluster for Jordan.wks. Points to cluster 10, which holds more data for the Jordan.wks file
9	999	First and last cluster containing Pick.wps
10	999	Last cluster of Jordan.wks

FIGURE D-25: Defragmenting a disk

Defragmenting a disk helps your computer operate more efficiently; consider using a defragmentation utility a couple of times per year to keep your computer running in top form

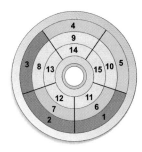

▲ On this fragmented disk, the purple, yellow, and blue files are stored in non-contiguous clusters

▲ When the disk is defragmented, the sectors of data for each file are moved to contiguous clusters

Remarkable advances in microprocessor technology have produced exponential increases in computer speed and power. In 1965, Gordon Moore, co-founder of chip-production giant Intel Corporation, predicted that the number of transistors on a chip would double every 18 to 24 months. Much to the surprise of engineers and Moore himself, "Moore's law" accurately predicted 30 years of chip development. In 1958, the first integrated circuit contained two transistors. The Pentium III Xeon processor, introduced in 1999, had 9.5 million transistors. The Pentium 4 processor, introduced only a year later, featured 42 million transistors.

What's really fascinating, though, is how these chips perform complex tasks simply by manipulating bits. How can pushing around 1s and 0s result in professional-quality documents, exciting action games, animated graphics, cool music, street maps, and e-commerce Web sites? To satisfy your curiosity about what happens deep in the heart of a microprocessor, you'll need to venture into the realm of instruction sets, fetch cycles, accumulators, and pointers.

A computer accomplishes a complex task by performing a series of very simple steps, referred to as instructions. An instruction tells the computer to perform a specific arithmetic, logical, or control operation. To be executed by a computer, an instruction must be in the form of electrical signals, those now-familiar 1s and 0s that represent "ons" and "offs." In this form, instructions are referred to as machine code. They are, of course, very difficult for people to read, so typically when discussing them, we use more understandable mnemonics, such as JMP, MI, and REG1.

An instruction has two parts: the op code and the operands. An op code, which is short for "operation code," is a command word for an operation such as add, compare, or jump. The operands for an instruction specify the data, or the address of the data, for the operation.

In the instruction JMP M1, the op code is JMP and the operand is M1. The op code JMP means jump or go to a different instruction. The operand M1 stands for the RAM address of the instruction to which the computer is supposed to go. The instruction JMP M1 has only one operand, but some instructions have more than one operand. For example, the instruction ADD REG1 REG2 has two operands: REG1 and REG2.

The list of instructions that a microprocessor is able to execute is known as its instruction set. This instruction set is built into the microprocessor when it is manufactured. Every task that a computer performs is determined by the list of instructions in its instruction set.

FIGURE D-26: The instruction cycle

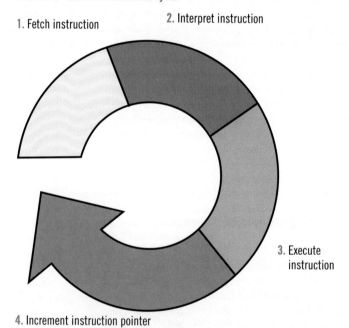

1. Fetch instruction

2. Interpret instruction

3. Execute instruction

4. Increment instruction pointer

The term **instruction cycle** refers to the process in which a computer executes a single instruction. Some parts of the instruction cycle are performed by the microprocessor's control unit; other parts of the cycle are performed by the ALU. The steps in this cycle are summarized in Figure D-26. Figure D-27 explains how the ALU, control unit, and RAM work together to process instructions.

FIGURE D-27: The ALU, the control unit, and RAM work to process instructions

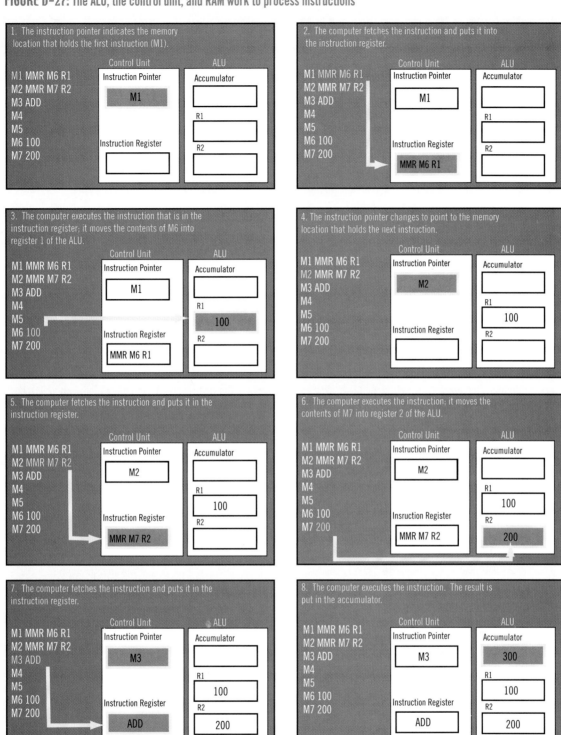

1. The instruction pointer indicates the memory location that holds the first instruction (M1).

M1 MMR M6 R1
M2 MMR M7 R2
M3 ADD
M4
M5
M6 100
M7 200

Control Unit
Instruction Pointer
M1
Instruction Register

ALU
Accumulator
R1
R2

2. The computer fetches the instruction and puts it into the instruction register.

M1 MMR M6 R1
M2 MMR M7 R2
M3 ADD
M4
M5
M6 100
M7 200

Control Unit
Instruction Pointer
M1
Instruction Register
MMR M6 R1

ALU
Accumulator
R1
R2

3. The computer executes the instruction that is in the instruction register; it moves the contents of M6 into register 1 of the ALU.

M1 MMR M6 R1
M2 MMR M7 R2
M3 ADD
M4
M5
M6 100
M7 200

Control Unit
Instruction Pointer
M1
Instruction Register
MMR M6 R1

ALU
Accumulator
R1
100
R2

4. The instruction pointer changes to point to the memory location that holds the next instruction.

M1 MMR M6 R1
M2 MMR M7 R2
M3 ADD
M4
M5
M6 100
M7 200

Control Unit
Instruction Pointer
M2
Instruction Register

ALU
Accumulator
R1
100
R2

5. The computer fetches the instruction and puts it in the instruction register.

M1 MMR M6 R1
M2 MMR M7 R2
M3 ADD
M4
M5
M6 100
M7 200

Control Unit
Instruction Pointer
M2
Instruction Register
MMR M7 R2

ALU
Accumulator
R1
100
R2

6. The computer executes the instruction; it moves the contents of M7 into register 2 of the ALU.

M1 MMR M6 R1
M2 MMR M7 R2
M3 ADD
M4
M5
M6 100
M7 200

Control Unit
Instruction Pointer
M2
Insruction Register
MMR M7 R2

ALU
Accumulator
R1
100
R2
200

7. The computer fetches the instruction and puts it in the instruction register.

M1 MMR M6 R1
M2 MMR M7 R2
M3 ADD
M4
M5
M6 100
M7 200

Control Unit
Instruction Pointer
M3
Instruction Register
ADD

ALU
Accumulator
R1
100
R2
200

8. The computer executes the instruction. The result is put in the accumulator.

M1 MMR M6 R1
M2 MMR M7 R2
M3 ADD
M4
M5
M6 100
M7 200

Control Unit
Instruction Pointer
M3
Instruction Register
ADD

ALU
Accumulator
300
R1
100
R2
200

Who Invented the Computer?

Just think how wealthy you would be if you had invented the computer, held a patent for its technology, and could collect even $1 in royalties for every computer ever sold. In 1973, a company called Sperry-Rand claimed to hold a patent on the technology for electronic digital computers. If the courts had upheld this claim, then no company would have been able to manufacture computers without obtaining a license from and paying royalties to Sperry-Rand. As you might expect, other computer companies, such as IBM, took issue with Sperry-Rand's claim. During the ensuing court battle, opposition lawyers suggested a surprising number of candidates as the "inventor" of the computer. You can read the brief sketches of these candidates and their machines, and then do some supplementary research on the Web, before deciding who you think invented the computer.

During the period 1821-1832, Charles Babbage drew up plans for a machine that he called the Analytical Engine. Like modern computers, this device was designed to be programmable. It would accept input from a set of punched cards that contained the instructions for performing calculations. The plans for the Analytical Engine called for it to store the results of intermediary calculations in a sort of memory. Results would be printed on paper. Babbage intended to power his device using a steam engine, which was the cutting-edge technology of his day. Unfortunately, Babbage worked on this machine for 11 years but never completed it.

In 1939, John Atanasoff began to construct a machine that came to be known as the Atanasoff-Berry Computer (ABC). Like today's computers, the ABC was powered by electricity, but it used vacuum tubes instead of integrated circuits. This machine was designed to accept input, store the intermediary results of calculations, and produce output. Unlike today's computers, the ABC was not a multipurpose machine. Instead, it was designed for a single purpose—finding solutions to systems of linear equations.

Atanasoff never completed the ABC, but he shared his ideas and technology with John Mauchly and J. Presper Eckert, who were working on plans for the ENIAC (Electronic Numerical Integrator and Computer). Like the ABC, the ENIAC was powered by electricity and used vacuum tubes for its computational circuitry. The machine could be "programmed" by rewiring its circuitry and it produced printed output. ENIAC went online in 1946. Eckert and Mauchly filed for a patent on their technology and formed a company that became Sperry-Rand.

The ENIAC was not originally designed to store a program in memory, along with data. The stored program concept—a key feature of today's computers—was proposed by John von Neumann, who visited the ENIAC project and then collaborated with Eckert and Mauchly on the EDVAC computer, which was completed in 1949. The EDVAC was an electronic, digital computer that could accept input, process data, store data and programs, and produce output. Like the ENIAC, the EDVAC used vacuum tubes for its computational circuitry. Whereas the ENIAC worked with decimal numbers, however, the EDVAC worked with binary numbers much like today's computers.

In 1938, German scientist Conrad Zuse developed a binary, digital computer called the Z-1. Zuse had designed his machine as a programmable, general-purpose device with input, storage, processing, and output capabilities. Unlike the ABC and ENIAC, the Z-1 was not a fully electronic device. Instead of using electrical signals to represent data, it used mechanical relays.

Zuse's work was cloaked in secrecy during World War II, and scientists in Allied countries had little or no knowledge of his technology. It is somewhat surprising, therefore, that a similar machine was constructed in the United States by Howard Aiken, who was working with funding from IBM. The Harvard Mark I, completed in 1944, was powered by electricity, but used mechanical relays for its computational circuitry.

No list of computer inventors would be complete without Alan Turing, who worked with a group of British scientists, mathematicians, and engineers to create a completely electronic computing device in 1943. Called the Colossus, Turing's machine was essentially a huge version of Atanasoff's ABC—a special-purpose device (designed to break Nazi codes) powered by electricity, with vacuum tubes for its computing circuitry.

The roster of possible computer "inventors" includes Babbage, Atanasoff, Eckert and Mauchly, von Neumann, Zuse, Aiken, and Turing. Patents were filed only by IBM for Aiken's Mark I and by Eckert and Mauchly for the ENIAC. Should any of these inventors be collecting royalties on computer technology?

▼ EXPAND THE IDEAS

1. The Sperry-Rand lawsuit ended with a ruling that the Eckert and Mauchly patent was not valid because the ENIAC inventors derived their ideas from Atanasoff. Do you think that this decision was correct? Write a one-page paper supporting your answer.

2. To be credited with the invention of the computer, do you think that the inventor should have been required to have completed a working model? Why or why not? Research patent information to provide background information on what is required.

3. What key components do you believe define a computer? Detail the specific characteristics that made the "computer" different from any other machine.

4. Research the development and invention of the automobile. What are the similarities between the invention of the automobile and the invention of the computer? Find several examples of articles, documentaries, or news stories. Write a summary of each article or media piece. Analyze your findings. Was the media voice consistent? Why or why not?

5. Do you know anyone who holds a patent and gets a royalty for an invention? If you don't know anyone personally, research a recent invention. What made it a unique invention and eligible for patent and royalty rights? Compile your findings into a poster presentation.

End of Unit Exercises

▼ KEY TERMS

ALU	Directory	Integrated circuit (IC)	Register
ASCII	EBCDIC	Kilobit	Reserved word
Benchmark	EPROM	Kilobyte	RIMM
Binary number system	Extended ASCII	Logical storage model	RISC
Bit	File Allocation Table (FAT)	Megabit	ROM
Byte	File date	Megabyte	ROM BIOS
Cache	File format	Megahertz (MHz)	Root directory
Capacitor	File management	Microprocessor	SDRAM
Character data	File management utility	Microprocessor clock	SEC cartridge
CISC	File size	Motherboard	Sectors
Cluster	File specification	Nanosecond	Serial processing
CMOS memory	File system	Native file format	SO-RIMM
Computer file	Filename	Numeric data	Subdirectory
Control unit	Filename extension	Parallel processing	Tracks
Data representation	File-naming conventions	Path	Unicode
Defragmentation utility	Folder	PGA	Virtual memory
Digital device	Fragmented file	Pipelining	Windows Explorer
Digital electronics	Gigahertz (GHz)	PROM	Word size
DIMM	Instruction cycle	RAM	
DIP	Instruction set	RDRAM	

▼ UNIT REVIEW

1. Review the bold terms in this unit. Then pick 10 terms that are most unfamiliar to you. Be sure that you can use your own words to define the terms you have selected.

2. Describe how the binary number system and binary coded decimals can use only 1s and 0s to represent numbers.

3. Describe the difference between numeric data, character data, and numerals. Then, list and briefly describe the four codes that computers typically use for character data.

4. Make sure that you understand the meaning of the following measurement terms; indicate what aspects of a computer system they are used to measure: KB, Kb, MB, Mb, GB, Kbps, MHz, GHz, ns.

5. List four types of memory and briefly describe how each one works.

6. Describe how the ALU and the control unit interact to process data.

7. Describe the difference between the Save and the Save As options provided by an application.

8. Explain the kinds of file management tasks that might best be accomplished using a file management utility such as Windows Explorer.

9. In your own words, describe the difference between a logical storage model and a physical storage model.

10. Make sure that you can describe what happens in the FAT when a file is stored or deleted.

▼ FILL IN THE BEST ANSWER

1. The _____ number system represents numeric data as a series of 0s and 1s.

2. ASCII is used primarily to represent _____ data.

3. Most personal computers use the _____ code to represent character data.

4. Digital _____ makes it possible for a computer to manipulate simple "on" and "off" signals to perform complex tasks.

5. An integrated _____ contains microscopic circuit elements, such as wires, transistors, and capacitors that are packed onto a very small square of semiconducting material.

6. The _____ in the microprocessor performs arithmetic and logical operations.

7. The _____ in the CPU directs and coordinates the operation of the entire computer system.

8. The timing in a computer system is established by the _____.

9. In RAM, microscopic electronic parts called _____ hold the electrical signals that represent data.

10. The instructions for the operations your computer performs when it is first turned on are permanently stored in _____.

11. System configuration information about the hard disk, date, and RAM capacity is stored in battery-powered _____ memory.

12. An operating system's file-naming _____ provide a set of rules for naming files.

13. A file _____ refers to the arrangement of data in a file and the coding scheme that is used to represent the data.

14. The main directory of a disk is sometimes referred to as the _____ directory.

15. A file's location is defined by a file _____, which includes the drive letter, folder(s), filename, and extension.

16. The file _____ can be important information when you've created several versions of a file and you want to know which version is the most recent.

17. The _____ option on an application's File menu allows you to name a file and specify its storage location.

18. A(n) _____ storage model helps you form a mental picture of how your files are arranged on a disk.

19. On a floppy disk or hard disk, data is stored in concentric circles called _____, which are divided into wedge-shaped _____.

20. Windows Explorer is an example of a file _____ utility.

▼ INDEPENDENT CHALLENGE 1

 The three leading manufacturers of processors are Intel, AMD, and Transmeta. These companies manufacture processors for personal computers as well as other devices.

1. Based on what you read in this unit, list and describe the factors that affect microprocessor performance. Create a table using the performance factors as column heads.

2. Use your favorite search engine on the Internet to research any two companies that produce microprocessors.

3. List their Web sites and any other pertinent contact information for the companies that you chose.

4. List three of the models that each company produces as row labels in the table you created in Step 1. Complete the table to show how these models rate, that is, their specifications for each performance factor.

5. Write a brief statement describing any new research or new products that each company is developing.

▼ INDEPENDENT CHALLENGE 2

 How quickly could you code a sentence using the Extended ASCII code? What is the history of coding and coding schemes? You can find a wealth of information about coding schemes that have been developed throughout the history of computing as well as coding used to transmit information.

1. Use your favorite search engine to research the history of Morse code. Write a brief paragraph outlining your findings.

2. Use the International Morse Code alphabet to write your full name.

3. Research the history of the ASCII code. Write a one-page summary of your findings.

4. Use the extended ASCII code to write your full name.

5. Research the history of the EBCDIC code. Write a one-page summary of your findings.

6. Use the extended EBCDIC code to write your full name.

▼ INDEPENDENT CHALLENGE 3

How will you organize the information that you store on your hard drive? Your hard disk will be your electronic filing cabinet for all your work and papers. You can create many different filing systems. The way you set up your folders will guide your work and help you keep your ideas and projects organized so you can work efficiently with your computer. Take some time to think about the work that you do, the types of documents or files you will be creating, and then decide how you will create files and folders.

1. Read each of the following plans for organizing files and folders on a hard disk and comment on the advantages and disadvantages of each plan.

    a. Create a folder for each file you create.

    b. Store all the files in the root directory.

    c. Store all files in the My Documents folder.

    d. Create a folder for each application you plan to use and store only documents you generate with that application in each folder.

    e. Create folders for broad topics such as memos, letters, budget, art, personal, and then store all related documents and files within those folders.

    f. Create folders based on specific topics such as tax, applications, household, school, then store all related documents and files within those folders.

    g. Create a new folder for each month and store all files or documents created in that month in that appropriate folder.

2. Write up a summary of how you plan to organize your hard disk and explain why you chose the method you did.

▼ INDEPENDENT CHALLENGE 4

You can use Windows Explorer or any file management program on your computer to explore and find specific files and folders on your hard disk.

1. Start Windows Explorer then expand the My Computer icon. List the devices under My Computer.

2. Open the My Documents folder on the Local Disk C: (if not available, find the folder that has your documents). List how many folders are in the My Documents folder on your hard disk.

3. Open one of the folders in the My Documents folder, then display the Details View. Are filename extensions showing? If so, list them and identify which programs would open those files.

4. How many different types of files can you find on your hard disk? List up to 10.

5. Make a list of five filenames that are valid under the file-naming conventions for your operating system. Create a list of five filenames that are not valid and explain the problem with each one.

6. Create five filenames that meet the file-naming conventions for Windows and for MAC OS. Then create five filenames that do not meet the file-naming conventions for Windows or for MAC OS, and explain why these filenames do not meet the file-naming conventions.

7. Pick any five files on the computer that you typically use, and write out the full path for each one. If you can, identify the programs that were used to create each of the files you found.

▼ VISUAL WORKSHOP

Your computer probably came with a specific amount of RAM. What if you wanted to upgrade to more RAM? How would you go about finding the RAM to purchase? How much RAM is enough? Is there too much RAM? Figure D-28 shows the Web page for Kingston Technology, a leading distributor and manufacturer of computer memory. You can use the Internet for researching and buying RAM. You will research RAM and determine the best buy for your system.

FIGURE D-28

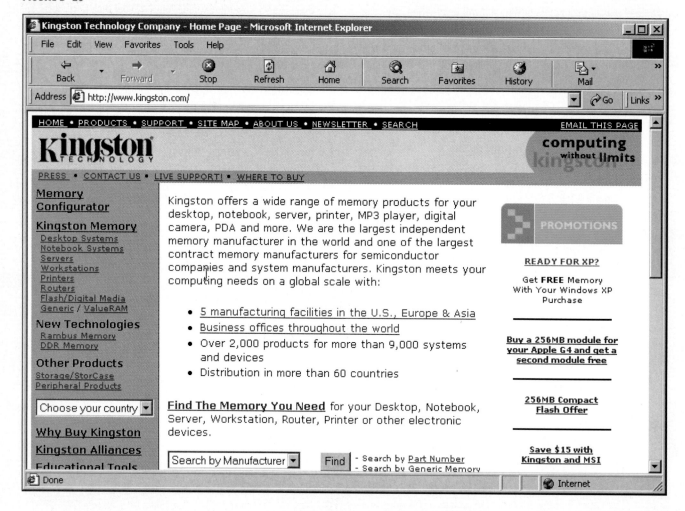

1. Use a search engine to search on RAM. What kinds of Web sites did you find? Did you need to be more specific in your search to find the RAM for your computer?

2. Complete a search on DRAM. Was this more successful in finding Web sites that would sell you chips to update the memory capacity on your computer?

3. Go to www.kingston.com, the page shown in Figure D-28, and click the link for the Memory Configurator. See if you can find the best memory for upgrading your system.

4. Write a brief summary of your findings.

5. Click the links for Desktop, Notebook, and then Server memory. Read the pages and write a brief summary of what you read for two of the links.

Glossary

Absolute reference ▶ In a worksheet formula, cell references (usually preceded by a $ symbol) that cannot change as a result of a move or copy operation.

Access time ▶ The estimated time for a storage device to locate data on a disk, usually measured in milliseconds.

Active matrix screen ▶ A type of LCD technology that produces a clear, sharp image because each pixel is controlled by its own transistor.

AGP (accelerated graphics port) ▶ An AGP is a type of interface, or slot, that provides a high-speed pathway for advanced graphics.

ALU (arithmetic logic unit) ▶ The part of the CPU that performs arithmetic and logical operations on the numbers stored in its registers.

Always-on connection ▶ A permanent connection, as opposed to a connection that is established and dropped as needed.

Analog device ▶ A device that operates on continuously varying data, such as a dimmer switch or a watch with a sweep second hand.

Application software ▶ Computer programs that help you perform a specific task such as word processing. Also called application programs, applications, or programs.

Archiving ▶ The process of moving infrequently used data from a primary storage device to a storage medium such as a CD-R.

ASCII (American Standard Code for Information Interchange) ▶ A code that represents characters as a series of 1s and 0s. Most computers use ASCII code to represent text, making it possible to transfer data between computers.

Automatic recalculation ▶ A feature found in spreadsheet software that automatically recalculates every formula after a user makes a change to any cell.

Beep code ▶ A series of audible beeps used to announce diagnostic test results during the boot process.

Benchmark ▶ A test used to measure computer hardware or software performance.

Binary digits ▶ Series of 1s and 0s representing data.

Binary number system ▶ A method for representing numbers using only two digits, 0 and 1; contrast this system to the decimal system, which uses ten digits: 0, 1, 2, 3, 4, 5, 6, 7, 8, and 9.

Bit ▶ A bit is the smallest unit of information handled by a computer. A bit can hold one of two values, either a 0 or a 1. Eight bits comprise a byte, which can represent a letter or number.

Bit depth ▶ The number of bits that determines the range of possible colors that can be assigned to each pixel. For example, an 8-bit color depth can create 256 colors. (Also called color depth.)

Boot process ▶ The sequence of events that occurs within a computer system between the time the user starts the computer and the time it is ready to process commands.

Bootstrap program ▶ A program stored in ROM that loads and initializes the operating system on a computer.

Browser ▶ A program that communicates with a Web server and displays Web pages.

Byte ▶ An 8-bit unit of information that represents a single character.

Cable ▶ Used to connect a peripheral device to a computer through a port.

Cable modem ▶ A communications device that can be used to connect a computer to the Internet via the cable TV infrastructure.

Cache ▶ Special high-speed memory that gives the CPU rapid access to data that would otherwise be accessed from disk. Also called RAM cache or cache memory.

Capacitor ▶ An electronic circuit component that stores an electrical charge; in RAM, a charged capacitor represents an "on" bit, and a discharged one represents an "off" bit.

CD-R ▶ An acronym for compact disc-recordable. CD-R is a type of optical disk technology that allows the user to create CD-ROMs and audio CDs.

CD-ROM drive ▶ A storage device that uses laser technology to read data from a CD-ROM.

CD-RW ▶ An acronym for compact disc-rewritable. CD-RW is a type of optical disk technology that allows the user to write data onto a CD, then change that data.

CD-writer ▶ A general term for recordable CD technologies such as CD-R and CD-RW.

Cell ▶ In spreadsheet terminology, the intersection of a column and a row. In cellular communications, a limited geographical area surrounding a cellular phone tower.

Cell reference ▶ The column letter and row number that designates the location of a worksheet cell. For example, the cell reference C5 refers to a cell in column C, row 5.

Character data ▶ Letters, symbols, or numerals that will not be used in arithmetic operations (name, social security number, etc.).

Chat group ▶ A discussion in which a group of people communicates online simultaneously.

CISC (complex instruction set computer) ▶ A general-purpose microprocessor chip designed to handle a wider array of instructions than a RISC chip.

Client ▶ A computer or software that requests information from another computer or server.

Clip art ▶ Graphics designed to be inserted into documents, Web pages, and worksheets, usually available in CD-ROM or Web-based collections.

Cluster ▶ A group of sectors on a storage medium that, when accessed as a group, speeds up data access.

CMOS (complementary metal oxide semiconductor) memory ▶ A type of battery-powered integrated circuit that holds semi-permanent configuration data.

Color depth ▶ The number of bits that determines the range of possible colors that can be assigned to each pixel. For example, an 8-bit color depth can create 256 colors. (Also called bit depth.)

Commercial software ▶ Copyrighted computer applications sold to consumers for profit.

Compiler ▶ Software that translates a program written in a high-level language into low-level instructions before the program is executed.

Computer ▶ A device that accepts input, processes data, stores data, and produces output.

Computer file ▶ A single collection of data stored on a storage medium.

Computer language ▶ A set of tools that allows a programmer to write instructions that a computer can execute.

Computer network ▶ A collection of computers and related devices, connected in a way that allows them to share data, hardware, and software.

Computer program ▶ A set of detailed, step-by-step instructions that tells a computer how to solve a problem or carry out a task.

Computer programmer ▶ A person who codes or writes computer programs.

Computer system ▶ The hardware, peripheral devices, and software working together to input data, process data, store data, and produce output.

Control unit ▶ The part of the ALU that directs and coordinates processing.

Controller ▶ A circuit board in a hard drive that positions the disk and read-write heads to locate data.

Copyright ▶ A form of legal protection that grants certain exclusive rights to the author of a program or the owner of the copyright.

Copyright notice ▶ A line such as "Copyright 2002 ACME Co." that identifies a copyright holder.

CPU (central processing unit) ▶ The main processing unit in a computer, consisting of circuitry that executes instructions to process data.

CRT (cathode ray tube) ▶ A display technology that uses a large vacuum tube similar to that used in television sets.

Cursor ▶ A symbol that marks the user's place on the screen and shows where typing will appear.

Cylinder ▶ A vertical stack of tracks that is the basic storage bin for a hard disk drive.

Data ▶ In the context of computing and data management, the symbols that a computer uses to represent facts and ideas.

Data bus ▶ An electronic pathway or circuit that connects the electronic components (such as the processor and RAM) on a computer's motherboard.

Data file ▶ A file containing words, numbers, or pictures that the user can view, edit, save, send, or print.

Data management software ▶ Software designed for tasks associated with maintaining and accessing data stored in data files.

Data module ▶ A file linked to a program and provides data necessary for certain functions of the program.

Data representation ▶ The use of electrical signals, marks, or binary digits to represent character, numeric, visual, or audio data.

Data transfer rate ▶ The amount of data that a storage device can move from a storage medium to computer memory in one second.

Database ▶ A collection of information that may be stored in more than one file.

Database management software ▶ Software developed for the task of manipulating data in the form of a database.

Defragmentation utility ▶ A software tool used to rearrange the files on a disk so that they are stored in contiguous clusters.

Desktop computer ▶ Computer small enough to fit on a desk and built around a single microprocessor chip.

Desktop operating system ▶ An operating system such as Windows ME or Mac OS X that is specifically designed for personal computers.

Desktop publishing software ▶ Software used to create high-quality output suitable for commercial printing. DTP software provides precise control over layout.

Device driver ▶ The software that provides the computer with the means to control a peripheral device.

Dial-up connection ▶ A connection that uses a phone line to establish a temporary Internet connection.

Digital ▶ Any system that works with discrete data, such as 0s and 1s, in contrast to analog.

Digital camera ▶ A input device that records an image in digital format.

Digital device ▶ A device that works with discrete (distinct or separate) numbers or digits.

Digital electronics ▶ Circuitry that's designed to work with digital signals.

Digitize ▶ The conversion of non-digital information or media to a digital format through the use of a scanner, sampler, or other input device.

DIMM (dual in-line memory module) ▶ A small circuit board that holds RAM chips. A DIMM has a 64-bit path to the memory chips.

DIP (dual in-line package) ▶ A chip configuration characterized by a rectangular body with numerous plugs along its edge.

Directory ▶ A list of files contained on a computer storage device.

Disk density ▶ The closeness of the particles on a disk surface. As density increases, the particles are packed more tightly together and are usually smaller.

Distribution disks ▶ One or more floppy disks or CDs that contain programs and data, which can be installed to a hard disk.

Document production software ▶ Computer programs that assist the user in composing, editing, designing, and printing documents.

DOS (disk operating system) ▶ The operating system software shipped with the first IBM PCs and used on millions of computers until the introduction of Microsoft Windows.

Dot matrix printer ▶ A printer that creates characters and graphics by striking an inked ribbon with small wires called "pins," generating a fine pattern of dots.

Dot pitch ▶ The diagonal distance between colored dots on a display screen. Measured in millimeters, dot pitch helps to determine the quality of an image displayed on a monitor.

Downloading ▶ The process of transferring a copy of a file from a remote computer to a local computer's disk drive.

DPI (dots per inch) ▶ Printer resolution as measured by the number of dots it can print per linear inch.

Drive bay ▶ An area within a computer system unit that can accommodate an additional storage device.

DSL (Digital Subscriber Line) ▶ A high-speed Internet connection that uses existing telephone lines, requiring close proximity to a switching station.

DSS (Digital Satellite System) ▶ A type of Internet connection that uses a network of satellites to transmit data.

DVD (digital video disc or digital versatile disc) ▶ An optical storage medium similar in appearance and technology to a CD-ROM but with higher storage capacity.

DVD drive ▶ An optical storage device that reads data from CD-ROM and DVD disks.

DVD-ROM ▶ A DVD disk that contains data that has been permanently stamped on the disk surface.

Dye sublimation printer ▶ An expensive, color-precise printer that heats ribbons containing color to produce consistent, photograph-quality images.

EBCDIC (Extended Binary-Coded Decimal Interchange Code) ▶ A method by which digital computers, usually mainframes, represent character data.

E-commerce (electronic commerce) ▶ Business connected over the Internet, including online shopping, linking businesses to businesses (sometimes called e-business or B2B), online stock trading, and electronic auctions.

EIDE (enhanced integrated drive electronics) ▶ A type of drive that features high storage capacity and fast data transfer.

E-mail (electronic mail) ▶ A single electronic message or the entire system of computers and software that handles electronic messages transmitted between computers over a communications network.

E-mail account ▶ A service that provides an e-mail address and mailbox.

E-mail address ▶ The unique address for each mailbox on the Internet, which typically consists of a user ID, an @ symbol, and the name of the computer that maintains the mailbox.

E-mail attachment ▶ A separate file that is transmitted along with an e-mail message.

E-mail client software ▶ Software that is installed on a client computer and has access to e-mail servers on a network. This software is used to compose, send, and read e-mail messages.

E-mail message ▶ A computer file containing a letter or memo that is transmitted electronically via a communications network.

E-mail server ▶ A computer that uses special software to store and send e-mail messages over the Internet.

E-mail system ▶ The collection of computers and software that works together to provide e-mail services.

EPROM (Erasable programmable read-only memory) ▶ ROM chips that can be erased and reused.

Exa- ▶ Prefix for a quintillion.

Executable file ▶ A file, usually with an .exe extension, containing instructions that tell a computer how to perform a specific task.

Expansion bus ▶ The segment of the data bus that transports data between RAM and peripheral devices.

Expansion card ▶ A circuit board that is plugged into a slot on a PC motherboard to add extra functions, devices, or ports.

Expansion port ▶ A socket into which the user plugs a cable from a peripheral device, allowing data to pass between the computer and the peripheral device.

Expansion slot ▶ A socket or slot on a PC motherboard designed to hold a circuit board called an expansion card.

Extended ASCII ► Similar to ASCII but with 8-bit character representation instead of 7-bit, allowing for an additional 128 characters.

Favorites ► A list of URLs for Web sites that you can create for your browser to store so that you can revisit those sites easily.

Field ► The smallest meaningful unit of information contained in a data file.

File ► A named collection of data (such as a computer program, document, or graphic) that exists on a storage medium, such as a hard disk, floppy disk, or CD-ROM.

File allocation table (FAT) ► A special file that is used by the operating system to store the physical location of all the files on a storage medium, such as a hard disk or floppy disk.

File format ► The method of organization used to encode and store data in a computer. Text formats include DOC and TXT. Graphics formats include BMP, TIFF, GIF, and PCX.

File management software ► Computer programs that help the user organize records, find records that match specific criteria, and print lists based on the information contained in records.

File management utility ► Software, such as Windows Explorer, that helps users locate, rename, move, copy, and delete files.

File size ► The physical size of a file on a storage medium, usually measured in kilobytes (KB).

File specification ► A combination of the drive letter, subdirectory, filename, and extension that identifies a file (for example, A:\word\filename.doc). Also called a path.

File structure ► A description of the way in which data is stored in a file.

File system ► A system that is used by an operating system to keep files organized.

File-naming conventions ► A set of rules established by the operating system that must be followed to create a valid filename.

Filename ► A set of letters or numbers that identifies a file.

Filename extension ► A set of letters and/or numbers added to the end of a filename that helps to identify the file contents or file type.

Flat file ► The electronic version of a box of index cards, each of which stores information about one entity, such as a person.

Floppy disk ► A removable magnetic storage medium, typically 3.5" in size, with a capacity of 1.44 MB.

Floppy disk drive ► A storage device that writes data on, and reads data from, floppy disks.

Folder ► The subdirectory, or subdivision, of a directory that can contain files or other folders.

Font ► A typeface or style of lettering, such as Arial, Times New Roman, and Gothic.

Formula ► In spreadsheet terminology, a combination of numbers and symbols that tells the computer how to use the contents of cells in calculations.

Fragmented file ► A file stored in scattered, noncontiguous clusters on a disk.

Frame ► An outline or boundary frequently defining a box. For document production software, a pre-defined area into which text or graphics may be placed.

Freeware ► Copyrighted software that is given away by the author or owner.

Fully justified ► The horizontal alignment of text in which the text terminates exactly at both margins of the document.

Function ► In worksheets, a built-in formula for making a calculation. In programming, a section of code that manipulates data but is not included in the main sequential execution path of a program.

Function key ► One of the keys numbered F1 through F12 located at the top of the computer keyboard that activates program specific commands.

Giga- ► Prefix for a billion.

Gigahertz (GHz) ► A measure of frequency equivalent to one billion cycles per second, usually used to measure speed.

Graphical user interface (GUI) ► A type of user interface that features on-screen objects, such as menus and icons, manipulated by a mouse. (Abbreviation is pronounced "gooey".)

Graphics ► Any pictures, photographs, or images that can be manipulated or viewed on a computer.

Graphics card ► A circuit board inserted into a computer to handle the display of text, graphics, animation, and videos. Also called a video card.

Graphics software ► Computer programs for creating, editing, and manipulating images.

Graphics tablet ► A device that accepts input from a pressure-sensitive stylus and converts strokes into images on the screen.

Handheld computer ► A small, pocket-sized computer designed to run on its own power supply and provide users with basic applications.

Hard disk ► See hard disk drive.

Hard disk drive ► A computer storage device that contains a large-capacity hard disk sealed inside the drive case. A hard disk is not the same as a 3.5" floppy disk that has a rigid plastic case.

Hard disk platter ► The component of a hard disk drive on which data is stored. It is a flat, rigid disk made of aluminum or glass and coated with a magnetic oxide.

Hardware ► The electronic and mechanical devices in a computer system.

Head crash ► A collision between the read-write head and the surface of the hard disk platter, resulting in damage to some of the data on the disk.

High-level language ► A computer language that allows a programmer to write instructions using human-like language.

History list ► A list that is created by your browser of the sites you visited so that you can display and track your sessions or revisit the site by clicking the URL in the list.

Home page ► In a Web site, the document that is the starting, or entry, page. On an individual computer, the Web page that a browser displays each time it is started.

Horizontal market software ► Any computer program that can be used by many different kinds of businesses (for example, an accounting program).

HTML (Hypertext Markup Language) ► A standardized format used to specify the format for Web page documents.

HTML tag ► An instruction, such as <B>...</B>, inserted into an HTML document to provide formatting and display information to a Web browser.

HTTP (Hypertext Transfer Protocol) ► The communications protocol used to transmit Web pages. HTTP:// is an identifier that appears at the beginning of most Web page URLs (for example, http://www.course.com).

Hypertext ► A way of organizing an information database by linking information through the use of text and multimedia.

IMAP (Internet Messaging Access Protocol) ► A protocol similar to POP that is used to retrieve e-mail messages from an e-mail server, but offers additional features, such as choosing which e-mails to download from the server.

Information ► The words, numbers, and graphics used as the basis for human actions and decisions.

Ink jet printer ► A non-impact printer that creates characters or graphics by spraying liquid ink onto paper or other media.

Input ► As a noun, "input" means the information that is conveyed to a computer. As a verb, "input" means to enter data into a computer.

Input device ► A device, such as a keyboard or mouse, that gathers input and transforms it into a series of electronic signals for the computer.

Install ► The process by which programs and data are copied to the hard disk of a computer system and otherwise prepared for access and use.

Installation agreement ► A version of the license agreement that appears on the computer screen when software is being installed and prompts the user to accept or decline.

Instant messaging ► A private chat in which users can communicate with each other.

Instruction cycle ► The steps followed by a computer to process a single instruction; fetch, interpret, execute, then increment the instruction pointer.

Instruction set ► The collection of instructions that a CPU is designed to process.

Integrated circuit (IC) ► A thin slice of silicon crystal containing microscopic circuit elements, such as transistors, wires, capacitors, and resistors; also called chips and microchips.

Internet ► The worldwide communication infrastructure that links computer networks using TCP/IP protocol.

Internet backbone ► The major communications links that form the core of the Internet.

Internet telephony ► A set of hardware and software that allows users to make phone-style calls over the Internet, usually without a long-distance charge.

Interpreter ► A program that converts high-level instructions in a computer program into machine language instructions, one instruction at a time.

IP address ► A unique identifying number assigned to each computer connected to the Internet.

ISA (Industry Standard Architecture) ► A standard for moving data on the expansion bus. Can refer to a type of slot, a bus, or a peripheral device. An older technology, it is rapidly being replaced by PCI architecture.

ISDN (Integrated Services Digital Network) ► A telephone company service that transports data digitally over dial-up or dedicated lines.

ISP (Internet Service Provider) ► A company that provides Internet access to businesses, organizations, and individuals.

Joystick ► A pointing input device used as an alternative to a mouse.

Kernel ► The core module of an operating system that typically manages memory, processes, tasks, and disks.

Keyboard ► An arrangement of letter, number, and special function keys that acts as the primary input device to the computer.

Keyboard shortcut ► The use of the [Alt] or the [Ctrl] key in combination with another key on the keyboard to execute a command, such as copy, paste, or cut.

Keyword ► A word or term used as the basis for a database or Web-page search.

Kilobit (Kbit or Kb) ► 1,024 bits.

Kilobyte (KB) ► Approximately 1,000 bytes; exactly 1,024 bytes.

LAN (local area network) ► An interconnected group of computers and peripherals located within a relatively limited area, such as a building or campus.

Land ► A non-pitted surface area on a CD that represents digital data.

Laser printer ► A printer that uses laser-based technology, similar to that used by photocopiers, to produce text and graphics.

LCD (liquid crystal display) ► A type of flat panel computer screen, typically found on notebook computers.

LCD screen ► See LCD.

Link ► Underlined text that allows users to jump between Web pages.

Linux ► A server operating system that is a derivative of UNIX and available as freeware.

Logical storage model ► Any visual aid or metaphor that helps a computer user visualize a file system.

Mac (Macintosh computer) ► A personal computer platform designed and manufactured by Apple Computer.

Mac OS ► The operating system software designed for use on Apple Macintosh and iMac computers.

Machine code ► Program instructions written in binary code that the computer can execute directly.

Machine language ► A low-level language written in binary code that the computer can execute directly.

Magnetic storage ► The recording of data onto disks or tape by magnetizing particles of an oxide-based surface coating.

Mailing list server ► Any computer and software that maintains a list of people who are interested in a topic and that facilitates message exchanges among all members of the list.

Main executable file ► A program that is used to start and run software, usually with an .exe file extension.

Mainframe computer ► A large, fast, and expensive computer generally used by businesses or government agencies to provide centralized storage processing and management for large amounts of data.

Megabit (Mb or Mbit) ► 1,048,576 bits.

Megabyte (MB) ► Approximately 1 million bytes; exactly 1,048,576 bytes.

Megahertz (MHz) ► A measure of frequency equivalent to 1 million cycles per second.

Memory ► The computer circuitry that holds data waiting to be processed.

Microcomputer ► A category of computer that is built around a single microprocessor chip.

Microprocessor ► An integrated circuit that contains the circuitry for processing data. It is a single-chip version of the central processing unit (CPU) found in all computers.

Microprocessor clock ► A device on the motherboard of a computer responsible for setting the pace of executing instructions.

Microsoft Windows ► An operating system developed by Microsoft Corporation that provides a graphical interface. Versions include Windows 3.1, Windows 95, Windows 98, Windows ME, Windows XP, Windows NT, and Windows 2000.

Millisecond (ms) ► A thousandth of a second.

MIME (Multipurpose Internet Mail Extension) ► A conversion process used for formatting non-ASCII messages so that they can be sent over the Internet.

Modem ► A device that sends and receives data to and from computers over telephone lines.

Modem card ► A device that provides a way to transmit data over phone lines or cable television lines.

Modifier key ► The [Ctrl], [Alt], or [Shift] key, used in conjunction with another key to expand the repertoire of available commands.

Monitor ► A display device that forms an image by converting electrical signals from the computer into points of colored light on the screen.

Motherboard ► The main circuit board in a computer that houses chips and other electronic components.

Mouse ► An input device that allows the user to manipulate objects on the screen by moving the mouse on the surface of a desk.

MP3 ► A file format that provides highly compressed audio files with very little loss of sound quality.

MP3 player ► Software that plays MP3 music files.

MPEG-2 ► A special type of data coding for movie files that are much too large to fit on a disk unless they are compressed.

Multitasking operating system ► An operating system that runs two or more programs at the same time.

Multiuser operating system ► An operating system that allows two or more users to run programs at the same time and use their own input/output devices.

Nanosecond ► A unit of time representing 1 billionth of a second.

Native file format ► A file format that is unique to a program or group of programs and has a unique file extension.

Natural language query ► A query using language spoken by human beings, as opposed to an artificially constructed language such as machine language.

Netiquette ► Internet etiquette or a set of guidelines for posting messages and e-mails in a civil, concise way.

Network card ► An expansion board mounted inside a computer to allow access to a local area network.

Network operating system ► Programs designed to control the flow of data, maintain security, and keep track of accounts on a network.

Newsgroup ► An online discussion group that centers around a specific topic.

Notation software ► Software used to help musicians compose, edit, and print musical scores.

Notebook computer ► Small, lightweight, portable computer that usually runs on batteries. Sometimes called laptop.

Numeric data ► Numbers that represent quantities and can be used in arithmetic operations.

Numeric keypad ► Calculator-style input devices for numbers located towards the right side of a keyboard.

Object code ► The low-level instructions that result from compiling source code.

Object-oriented database ► A database model that organizes data into classes of objects that can be manipulated by programmer-defined methods.

Online ▶ Refers to being connected to the Internet.

Op code (operation code) ▶ An assembly language command word that designates an operation, such as add (ADD), compare (CMP), or jump (JMP).

Open source software ▶ Software, such as Linux, that includes its uncompiled source code, which can be modified and distributed by programmers.

Operand ▶ The part of an instruction that specifies the data, or the address of the data, on which the operation is to be performed.

Operating system (OS) ▶ Software that controls the computer's use of its hardware resources, such as memory and disk storage space.

Optical storage ▶ A means of recording data as light and dark spots on a CD, DVD, or other optical media.

Output ▶ The results produced by a computer (for example, reports, graphs, and music).

Output device ▶ A device, such as a monitor or printer, that displays, prints, or transmits the results of processing from the computer memory.

Packet ▶ A small unit of data transmitted over a network or the Internet.

Page layout ▶ The physical positions of elements on a document page, such as headers, footers, page numbers, and graphics.

Parallel port ▶ Commonly used to connect most printers to a computer; however some printers are designed to connect to a USB port or a serial port.

Parallel processing ▶ A technique by which two or more processors in a computer perform processing tasks simultaneously.

Passive matrix screen ▶ A display found on older notebook computers that relies on timing to ensure that the liquid crystal cells are illuminated.

Password ▶ A special set of symbols used to restrict access to a computer or network.

Path ▶ A file's location in a file structure. (See File specification.)

PC ▶ A microcomputer that uses Windows software and contains an Intel-compatible microprocessor.

PC card ▶ A credit card-sized circuit board used to connect a modem, memory, network card, or storage device to a notebook computer.

PCI (Peripheral Component Interconnect) ▶ A method for transporting data on the expansion bus. Can refer to type of data bus, expansion slot, or transport method used by a peripheral device.

PCMCIA (Personal Computer Memory Card International Association) slot ▶ An external expansion slot typically found on notebook computers.

PDA (Personal Digital Assistant) ▶ A computer that is smaller and more portable than a notebook computer (also called a palm-top computer).

Peripheral device ▶ A component or equipment, such as a printer or scanner, that expands a computer's input, output, or storage capabilities.

Personal computer ▶ A microcomputer designed for use by an individual user for applications such as Internet browsing and word processing.

PGA (pin-grid array) ▶ A common chip design used for microprocessors.

Physical storage model ▶ The way data is stored on a storage media.

Pipelining ▶ A technology that allows a processor to begin executing an instruction before completing the previous instruction.

Pit ▶ Dark spot that is burned onto the surface of a CD to represent digital data.

Pixel (picture element) ▶ The smallest unit in a graphic image. Computer display devices use a matrix of pixels to display text and graphics.

Platform ▶ A family or category of computers based on the same underlying software and hardware.

Plug and Play ▶ The ability of a computer to recognize and adjust the system configuration for a newly added device automatically.

POP (Post Office Protocol) ▶ A protocol that is used to retrieve e-mail messages from an e-mail server.

POP server ▶ A computer that receives and stores e-mail data until retrieved by the e-mail account holder.

PostScript ▶ A printer language developed by Adobe Systems that uses a special set of commands to control page layout, fonts, and graphics.

Power-on self-test (POST) ▶ A diagnostic process that runs during startup to check components of the computer, such as the graphics card, RAM, keyboard, and disk drives.

Presentation software ▶ Software that provides tools to combine text, graphics, graphs, animation, and sound into a series of electronic "slides" that can be output on a projector, or as overhead transparencies, paper copies, or 35-millimeter slides.

Printer ▶ A peripheral device used to create hard copy output.

Printer Control Language (PCL) ▶ A standard language used to send page formatting instructions from a computer to a laser or ink jet printer.

Processing ▶ The manipulation of data using a systematic series of actions.

Project management software ▶ Software specifically designed as a tool for planning, scheduling, and tracking projects and their costs.

PROM (programmable read-only memory) ▶ Memory that can be created using a special machine through a process called burning.

Public domain software ▶ Software that is available for use by the public without restriction, except that it cannot be copyrighted.

Query ▶ A search specification that prompts the computer to look for particular records in a file.

Query by example (QBE) ▶ A type of database interface in which users fill in a field with an example of the type of information that they are seeking.

Query language ▶ A set of command words that can be used to direct the computer to create databases, locate information, sort records, and change the data in those records.

RAID (redundant array of independent disks) ▶ Disks used by mainframes and microcomputers in which many disk platters provide data redundancy for faster data access and increased protection from media failure.

RAM (random access memory) ▶ A type of computer memory circuit that holds data, program instructions, and the operating system while the computer is on.

Random access ▶ The ability of a storage device (such as a disk drive) to go directly to a specific storage location without having to search sequentially from a beginning location.

RDRAM (Rambus dynamic RAM) ▶ A fast (up to 600 MHz) type of memory used in newer personal computers.

Read-write head ▶ The mechanism in a disk drive that magnetizes particles on the storage disk surface to write data, or senses the bits that are present to read data.

Record ▶ In the context of database management, a record is the set of fields of data that pertain to a single entity in a database.

Register ▶ A scratch pad area of the ALU and control unit where data or instructions are moved so that they can be processed.

Relational database ▶ A database structure incorporating the use of tables that can establish relationships with other similar tables.

Relative reference ▶ In a worksheet, cell references that can change if cells change position as a result of a move or copy operation.

Reserved word ▶ Special words used as commands in some operating systems that may not be used in filenames.

Resolution ▶ The density of the grid used to display or print text and graphics; the greater the horizontal and vertical density, the higher the resolution.

RIMM (Rambus in-line memory module) ▶ A memory module using RDRAM.

RISC (reduced instruction set computer) ▶ A microprocessor chip designed for rapid and efficient processing of a small set of simple instructions.

ROM (read-only memory) ▶ One or more integrated circuits that contain permanent instructions that the computer uses during the boot process.

ROM BIOS (basic input/output system) ▶ A small set of basic input/output system instructions stored in ROM that causes the computer system to load critical operating files when the user turns on the computer.

Root directory ▶ The main directory of a disk.

Router ▶ A device found at each intersection on the Internet backbone that examines the IP address of incoming data and forwards the data towards its destination. Also used by LANs.

Safe Mode ▶ A menu option that appears when Windows is unable to complete the boot sequence. By entering Safe Mode, a user can gracefully shut down the computer then try to reboot it.

Scanner ▶ An input device that converts a printed page of text or images into a digital format.

Script ▶ Program that contains a list of commands that are automatically executed as needed.

SCSI (small computer system interface) ▶ An interface standard used for attaching peripheral devices, such as disk drives. Pronounced "scuzzy."

SDRAM (synchronous dynamic RAM) ▶ A type of RAM that synchronizes itself with the CPU, thus enabling it to run at much higher clock speeds than conventional RAM.

Search engine ▶ Program that uses keywords to find information on the Internet and return a list of relevant documents.

Search operator ▶ A word or symbol that has a specific function within a search, such as "AND" or "+".

SEC (single edge contact) cartridge ▶ A common, cassette-like chip design for microprocessors.

Sectors ▶ Subdivision of the tracks on a storage medium that provide a storage area for data.

Sequential access ▶ A form of data storage, usually on computer tape, that requires a device to read or write data one record after another, starting at the beginning of the medium.

Serial processing ▶ Processing of data that completes one instruction before beginning another.

Server ▶ A computer or software on a network that supplies the network with data and storage.

Server software ▶ Software used by servers to locate and distribute data requested by Internet users.

Setup program ▶ A program module supplied with a software package for the purpose of installing the software.

Shareware ▶ Copyrighted software marketed under a license that allows users to use the software for a trial period and then send in a registration fee if they wish to continue to use it.

Shrink-wrap license ▶ A legal agreement printed on computer software packaging that goes into effect when the package is opened.

Single-user operating system ▶ A type of operating system that is designed for one user at a time with one set of input and output devices.

SMTP (Simple Mail Transfer Protocol) server ▶ A computer used to send e-mail across a network or the Internet.

Software ▶ The instructions that prepare a computer to do a task, indicate how to interact with a user, and specify how to process data.

Software license ▶ A legal contract that defines how a user may use a computer program.

SO-RIMM (small outline Rambus in-line memory module) ▶ A small memory module that contains RDRAM, used primarily in notebook computers.

Sound card ▶ A circuit board that gives the computer the ability to accept audio input from a microphone, play sound files stored on disks and CD-ROMs, and produce audio output through speakers or headphones.

Source code ▶ Computer instructions written in a high-level language.

Speakers ▶ Output devices that receive signals for the computer's sound card to play music, narration, or sound effects.

Spreadsheet ▶ A numerical model or representation of a real situation, presented in the form of a table.

Spreadsheet software ▶ Software for creating electronic worksheets that hold data in cells and perform calculations based on that data.

SQL (Structured Query Language) ▶ A popular query language used by mainframes and microcomputers.

Storage ▶ The area in a computer where data is retained on a permanent basis.

Storage device ▶ A mechanical apparatus that records data to and retrieves data from a storage medium.

Storage medium ▶ The physical material used to store computer data, such as a floppy disk, a hard disk, or a CD-ROM.

Store-and-forward technology ▶ A technology used by communications networks in which an e-mail message is temporarily held in storage on a server until it is requested by a client computer.

Stored program ▶ A set of instructions that resides on a storage device, such as a hard drive, and can be loaded into memory and executed.

Structured file ▶ A file that consists of a collection of records, each with the same set of fields.

Subdirectory ▶ A directory found under the root directory.

Supercomputer ▶ The fastest and most expensive type of computer, capable of processing more than 1 trillion instructions per second.

SuperDisk ▶ A storage technology manufactured by Imation. Disks have a capacity of 120 MB and require special disk drives; a standard floppy disk drive will not read them. However, they are backward-compatible with standard floppy disk technology, which means you can use a SuperDisk drive to read and write to standard floppy disks.

Support module ▶ A file that can be called by the main executable program to provide auxiliary instructions or routines.

System requirements ▶ Specifications for the operating system and hardware configuration necessary for a software product to work correctly. The criteria that must be met for a new computer system or software product to be a success.

System software ▶ Computer programs that help the computer carry out essential operating tasks.

System unit ▶ The case or box that contains the computer's power supply, storage devices, main circuit board, processor, and memory.

Table ▶ An arrangement of data in a grid of rows and columns. In a relational database, a collection of record types with their data.

Tape backup ▶ A copy of data from a computer's hard disk, stored on magnetic tape and used to restore lost data.

Tape cartridge ▶ A removable magnetic tape module similar to a cassette tape.

TCP/IP (Transmission Control Protocol/Internet Protocol) ▶ A standard set of communication rules used by every computer that connects to the Internet.

Tera- ▶ Prefix for a trillion.

TFT (thin film transistor) ▶ An active matrix screen that updates rapidly and is essential for crisp display of animations and video.

Thermal transfer printer ▶ An expensive, color-precise printer that uses wax containing color to produce numerous dots of color on plain paper.

Toggle key ▶ A key that switches back and forth between two modes, such as Caps Lock on or Caps Lock off.

Touchpad ▶ An alternative input device often found on notebook computers.

Track point ▶ An alternative input device often found on notebook computers.

Trackball ▶ Pointing input device used as an alternative to a mouse.

Tracks ▶ A series of concentric or spiral storage areas created on a storage medium during the formatting process.

UDMA (Ultra DMA) ▶ A faster version of DMA technology.

Ultra ATA ▶ A disk drive technology that is an enhanced version of EIDE. Also referred to as Ultra DMA or Ultra IDE.

Unicode ▶ A 16-bit character representation code that can represent more than 65,000 characters.

Uninstall routine ▸ A program that removes software files, references, and Windows Registry entries from a computer's hard disk.

UNIX ▸ A multi-user, multitasking server operating system developed by AT&T's Bell Laboratories in 1969.

Unzipped ▸ Refers to files that have been uncompressed.

Uploading ▸ The process of sending a copy of a file from a local computer to a remote computer.

URL (Uniform Resource Locator) ▸ The address of a Web page.

Usenet ▸ A worldwide Internet bulletin board system of newsgroups that share common topics.

User ID ▸ A combination of letters and numbers that serves as a user's identification. Also referred to as a user name.

User interface ▸ The software and hardware that enable people to interact with computers.

Utility ▸ A subcategory of system software designed to augment the operating system by providing ways for a computer user to control the allocation and use of hardware resources.

Value ▸ A number used in a calculation.

Vertical market software ▸ Computer programs designed to meet the needs of a specific market segment or industry, such as medical record-keeping software.

Videogame console ▸ A computer specifically designed for playing games using a television screen and game controllers.

Viewable image size (vis) ▸ A measurement of the maximum image size that can be displayed on a monitor screen.

Virtual memory ▸ A computer's use of hard disk storage to simulate RAM.

Voice band modem ▸ The type of modem that would typically be used to connect a computer to a telephone line. See Modem.

Volatile ▸ Data that can exist only with a constant power supply.

Web (World Wide Web) ▸ An Internet service that links documents and information from computers distributed all over the world using the HTTP protocol.

Web page ▸ A document on the World Wide Web that consists of a specially coded HTML file with associated text, audio, video, and graphics files. A Web page often contains links to other Web pages.

Web server ▸ A computer that uses special software to transmit Web pages over the Internet.

Web site ▸ Location on the World Wide Web that contains information relating to specific topics.

Web-based e-mail ▸ An e-mail account that stores, sends, and receives e-mail on a Web site rather than a user's computer.

Windows Explorer ▸ A file management utility included with most Windows operating systems that helps users manage their files.

Windows Registry ▸ A crucial data file maintained by the Windows operating system that contains the settings needed by a computer to correctly use any hardware and software that has been installed on the system. Also called the Registry.

Word processing software ▸ Computer programs that assist the user in producing documents, such as reports, letters, papers, and manuscripts.

Word size ▸ The number of bits a CPU can manipulate at one time, which is dependent on the size of the registers in the CPU and the number of data lines in the bus.

Worksheet ▸ A computerized, or electronic, spreadsheet.

Workstation ▸ (1) A computer connected to a local area network. (2) A powerful desktop computer designed for specific tasks.

Write-protect window ▸ A small hole and sliding cover on a floppy disk that restricts writing to the disk.

Zip disk ▸ Floppy disk technology manufactured by Iomega available in 100 MB and 250 MB versions.

Zipped ▸ Refers to files that have been compressed.

Index

groupware software, 82

GUI (graphical user interface), 70, 71

H

handheld computers, 6–7

hard drive(s)

  basic description of, 8–9, 35

  platters, 42, 43

  storing files on, 118–119

  technology, 42–43

hardware. *See also specific hardware*

  basic description of, 2, 33–64

  platforms and, 12

Harvard Mark I computer, 122, 123

head crashes, 42

headers, 74

headphone jacks, 45

help, 71

Hewlett-Packard, 12, 59

HFS (Macintosh Hierarchical File System), 118

high-level languages, 68

History list, 20

HKEY_CURRENT_CONFIG key, 57

.hlp extension, 67

home pages, 18, 20

horizontal market software, 82

.htm extension, 10

HTML (HyperText Markup Language), 20–21. HTML tags (listed by name)

  basic description of, 18

  e-mail and, 22

  frames, 74–75

HTTP (HyperText Transfer Protocol), 18–19, 194–195, 200–201, 210

hypertext, 18

I

IBM (International Business Machines)

  Harvard Mark I computer, 122, 123

  mainframes, 7, 98

  PCs (personal computers), 12, 59, 72

icons, 73, 118, 119

iMac, 12, 84. *See also* Macintosh

IMAP (Internet Messaging Access Protocol), 22

information, use of the term, 10

ink jet printers, 51–52

input, use of the term, 4. *See also* input devices

input devices. *See also* keyboards; mouse

  basic description of, 2

insertion point, 52

installation, 86–89

instant messaging, 14

instructions, 120–121

integrated circuits (ICs), 100

Intel, 103

intellectual property, 86–87

Internet. *See also* World Wide Web

  always-on connections to, 16

  backbone, 14–15

  basic description of, 14–15

  broadcasts, 14

  connecting to, 16–17

  dial-up connections to, 16

  downloading data from, 14–15

  groupware and, 82

  radio, 14

  telephony, 14

  uploading data to, 14–15

Internet Explorer browser (Microsoft), 20, 88

interpreters, 68–69

Iomega, 40

IP (Internet Protocol), 14

ISA (industry standard architecture) slots, 46–47

ISDN (Integrated Services Digital Network), 16

  basic description of, 16–17

  e-mail and, 26

  POP servers and, 22–23

iTunes, 84

J

Japan, 58, 90

Java, 68

joystick, 54–55

JPEG (Joint Photographics Experts Group) format, 108

K

KDE (K Desktop Environment), 73

keyboards, 8–9, 52–53

keywords, 20

kilobits, 99

kilobytes, 99

Korea, 90

L

labels, 76

LANs (local area networks), 2, 6

laser

  lens, 45

  light, 36

  printers, 51–52

LCD (liquid crystal display), 48

license agreements, 86–87, 89

link(s). *See also* URLs (uniform resource locators)

  appearance of, as underlined text, 19, 21

  basic description of, 18

Linux, 12, 72–73

logging on, 16

logical

  storage models, 114–115

"look and feel," of software, 70

M

Macintosh, 12–13

  audio editing software, 84

  file management and, 112–113, 118

  Finder, 113

  FireWire ports, 55

  iMac, 12, 84

  iTunes, 84

  operating system, revisions to, 72

  software installation and, 88

  user interface, 72

machine language, 68–69

magnetic storage, 36, 38

mailing list servers, 14

main circuit board (motherboard), 8, 100–101

main executable file, 66

mainframe computers, 6, 7, 98

MathCAD, 82

Mathematica, 82–83

mathmatical modeling software, 82

Mauchly John, 122, 123

Media Player, 88

megabit, 99

megabytes, 99, 104

megahertz, 102, 104

memory. *See also* RAM (random access memory)
  basic description of, 4–5, 106–107
  boot process and, 24
  cache, 102
  CMOS, 56, 106–107
  creating files and, 116
  display devices and, 48
  leaks, 70
  loading applications into, 116
  output devices and, 2
  read-only (ROM), 8, 24, 101, 106–107
  stored programs and, 5
  types, difference between, 107
  video, 48
  virtual, 106–107

microcomputers, 6. *See also* PCs (personal computers)

microprocessors, 46, 70, 120–121
  basic description of, 4–5, 101–103
  boot process and, 24
  clock speed of, 102
  RAM and, 104
  supercomputers and, 6

Microsoft Excel, 108

Microsoft Internet Explorer browser, 20, 88

Microsoft Office, 90

Microsoft Visual Basic, 68

Microsoft Visual Basic Scripting Edition (VBScript), 68

Microsoft Windows
  basic description of, 12, 72
  boot process and, 25
  device drives and, 54–55
  Explorer, 71, 112, 114–115
  File Manager, 113
  interface, 13, 73
  keyboard shortcuts, 52
  Media Player, 88
  My Computer feature, 114
  platform, 12–13
  Registry, 56–57, 88
  software installation and, 88
  utilities, 70–71

Microsoft Word, 75, 108, 116–117

Microsoft XBox, 6

MIDI (Musical Instrument Digital Interface), 84. *See also* sound

MindTwister Math, 84

modems, 46
  basic description of, 8–9, 17
  dial-up connections and, 16

modifier keys, 52–53

monitor(s)
  basic description of, 8–9, 48–49
  size of, 48–49

Moore, Gordon, 120

Moore's Law, 120

motherboard (main circuit board), 8, 100–101

mouse, 8–9

MP3 format, 84. *See also* sound

MPEG (Motion Picture Experts Group), 44

multifunction devices, 54–55

multitasking operating systems, 72

multiuser operating systems, 72

My Computer, 114

N

nanoseconds, 104

National Safety Council, 58

native file formats, 108

netiquette, 22

network(s)
  basic description of, 2
  cards, 16, 46
  local area (LANs), 2, 6
  operating system (NOS), 72

Neumann, John von, 122, 123

newsgroups, 14

Nintendo, 6

Nortel, 59

NOS (network operating systems), 72

notation software, 84

notebook computers, 39, 46–49, 54
  basic description of, 6–7
  boot process and, 25

NTFS (Windows NT File System), 118

numeric
  data, 34, 98
  keypad, 52–53

0

object
  code, 68
  -oriented databases, 78

Omnibus Crime Control and Safe Streets Act, 26

online, use of the term, 16

Open dialog box, 112

operating system(s). *See also specific operating systems*
  basic description of, 70–71
  boot process and, 24
  classification of, as system software, 12
  comparing, 72–73
  crashes, 70
  file management and, 110, 112–113
  software installation and, 88

optical
  storage, 36–37

output devices, basic description of, 2, 4–5. *See also* monitors; printers

P

packets, 14

page layout, 74

paint software, 80–81

Web page(s). *See also* HTML (HyperText Markup Language); World Wide Web

authoring software, 74–75

basic description of, 18

containing frames, 74–75

home pages, 18, 20

underlined text on, indicating links, 19, 21

Web server(s), 18. *See also* servers

e-commerce and, 121

names, in URLs, 19

Windows (Microsoft)

basic description of, 12, 72

boot process and, 25

device drives and, 54–55

Explorer, 71, 112, 114–115

File Manager, 113

interface, 13, 73

keyboard shortcuts, 52

Media Player, 88

My Computer feature, 114

platform, 12–13

Registry, 56–57, 88

software installation and, 88

utilities, 70–71

WinZip, 88, 108

Word (Microsoft), 75, 108, 116–117

word processing software, 74–75, 116. *See also* Word (Microsoft)

worksheets, 76–77

workstations, 6

World War II, 122

World Wide Web. *See also* Web pages; Web servers

basic description of, 18–19

-based e-mail, 22

search engines and, 20–21

technology, 194–195

URLs (uniform resource locators) and, 18–20

write-protect window, 40–41

X

Xerox, 59, 72

.xls extension, 108

Z

.zip extension, 108

ZIP drives, 35, 40–41

Zuse, Conrad, 122, 123